AS YOU GO

TIFFANY DAVIS

WESTBOW
PRESS®
A DIVISION OF THOMAS NELSON
& ZONDERVAN

WestBow Press books may be ordered through booksellers or by contacting:

WestBow Press
A Division of Thomas Nelson & Zondervan
1663 Liberty Drive
Bloomington, IN 47403
www.westbowpress.com
844-714-3454

ISBN: 978-1-6642-0397-6 (sc)
ISBN: 978-1-6642-0399-0 (hc)
ISBN: 978-1-6642-0398-3 (e)

Library of Congress Control Number: 2020916781

Print information available on the last page.

WestBow Press rev. date: 09/14/2020

CONTENTS

FOREWORD – THE START OF ME

I asked God to "burn me beautiful." I wanted him to peel off all of those layers that were holding me back, get rid of all those lies that I had believed about myself, and raise me up to be the woman of God he had created me to be.

A few years back, my dad passed away suddenly from a heart attack, and I found myself asking a question: "Do I want to sit here and be really sad, or do I want to run after God?" I decided for myself and for my family that I had no choice but to run after God ("If from there you seek the Lord your God, you will find him if you seek him with all your heart and with all your soul"—Deuteronomy 4:29, NIV). I began seeking him with my whole heart. I went up for every altar call, and I started reading my Bible, journaling, and going on "prayer walks."

One day when I was in church, I felt like a lightning bolt was setting me on fire. I couldn't stop crying and shaking, and I felt the presence of God as I never had before. I just wanted to pray for people. I realized at that moment that I was changed; I had a fire burning in me that I didn't have before. The Bible started coming alive to me, and suddenly everything but pursuing God seemed trivial. After this experience, we had a series of guest speakers come in, and I had the same lightning bolt experience of his presence.

It would leave me on the ground weeping every time. God was putting a fire in me that would never burn out.

God showed me the importance of John 15 in the Bible. I spent a lot of my life not connected to Jesus, and not spending time with God was causing me to wither. I cared more about the things of this world than about the things of God, so in return, I was full of fear, depression, worry, and a whole slew of other feelings. But the moment I made that decision to run after him and stay and live in a lifestyle of being connected to the vine (to him), he began bringing me on a journey of showing me new things all the time. I see myself constantly growing and changing, becoming a person that I barely recognize. The old me has been shed, and my Father is making me into a new creation full of boldness, and slowly he is bringing me into my destiny.

Raising three daughters has been the most valued task I have ever been asked to do. Watching my girls grow into beautiful women has brought me endless joy. I feel that God has blessed me with not only three daughters but three friends. I have learned much about life from raising my girls, and I wanted to pass down these lessons to the next generation.

I have always felt that my most important role as a mom is to teach my girls about Jesus. I didn't want them just to know a bunch of facts about God; I wanted them to encounter him and have a real relationship with him. My goal was for them to know that when you put your life in God's hands, your life is filled with much more peace and purpose. I want my girls to see my life as an example of a life that has been completely turned around by the power of God. I want my girls to taste and see that he is good.

I have always been a big fan of daily devotionals. Daily devotionals are an excellent tool in helping my daily quiet time with Jesus. As I send my girls off into the world, I want to equip them with a tool that can help build a daily relationship with Jesus.

As you draw near to God, you can build up your own lessons that Jesus shows you. This book can be used during the different stages of your life. I have learned new lessons during each season I have lived through, so I am hoping you will take the nuggets of wisdom that I have learned and use them to grow your own faith. Take it and run! Live an empowered life! Don't ever live your life with a victim mentality; live a life of power. Run after God! Teach your kids about Jesus; it's the way, the truth, and the only way to live. You got this! In this process, I want to share my journey of learning and growing, and hopefully it will encourage you in your walk with God. What a wonderful journey this is!

1

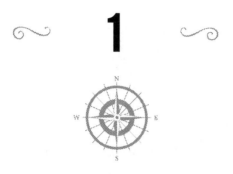

THE WORD

The other day, I was struggling with thoughts of insecurity. A negative thought entered into my head. And I believed that lie. Pretty soon, I couldn't think about anything else. I thought everyone was judging me and thinking badly of me. I kept asking God to take away my negative thoughts and to give me peace. For a couple of days, I was stuck in my negative thoughts.

I finally sat down with my Bible and decided to start reading until God spoke to me through his scripture. I read for a while until I got to Matthew 5:15, which says not to put a light under a basket but to place it on a stand for everyone to see. In the moment, that verse came alive to me. It pierced me right in the heart. I knew that God was speaking to me. The reason why I was struggling was because I had preached at church and was worried I hadn't said the right thing. When I got that word in my Bible, all of my negative thoughts broke, and all I cared about was that God was proud I had shined my light.

How about we treat the Bible as though it is actually God's Word, ready to speak into our lives? Hebrews 4:12 says that the Word of God is alive and active. Many people treat the Bible like a nice history lesson instead of praying that God illuminate his words to speak straight to the heart. I like to sit down with a pen, waiting to underline and note what part of the reading is speaking to me. I'll pray ahead of time for the Holy Spirit to encounter me as I read. I pray for God to speak to me through the Word.

When I first started growing as a Christian, I would just read a short devotional and the verse that went with it and then call it good while checking it off my list. That's okay, but if you see the Bible as God's actual Word, then you will be hungry for more. You will treat it as real food for your soul, which you can't get enough of. So why not keep reading? Read until that verse stands out to you. The more you eat, the more you grow. Ask God for passion for his Word. Nothing brings more freedom than God's Word spoken straight to your heart.

Father, I pray that your Word would come alive to me. I pray that you would give me a passion and desire to read the Bible. I thank you that it is alive, and I pray that the words will pop off the page for me. Help me to grow, to be strengthened, and to live a life of freedom. I pray that I will be able to hear clearly what you have for me. I thank you that your word is a lamp unto my feet and a light unto my path. Amen.

2

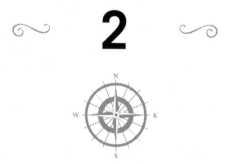

MESSAGE TO THE DAUGHTERS

I was walking out the door this morning, juggling my coffee and my ultra-wiggly dog, and trying to put on a hooded coat. My hair was extra frizzy because there was no time to straighten it before school drop-off. I found a hood to squish down my afro and started walking down my stairs with half my hair contained and the rest bulging around my hood like a lion's mane. As I was walking down the stairs, there was a girl walking down the street who stopped and took a picture of me when she saw me. I laughed inwardly at the thought that I must look pretty ridiculous.

I then I thought about a problem with social media that I never realized before. The girls must feel like they *always* have to look put together—hair and makeup done—because you never know when someone is going to take a picture of you. These kids are constantly taking pictures of everyone and everything. So you never know when you are going to be the star of their social media story. No more sweatpants and roll-out-of-bed days; every day you are a movie star. I just laughed this off, but it made me wonder how it might affect others who have zero self-confidence. I had already noticed a lot of the other problems. One of the biggest issues I noticed was that every day the kids were continually taking pictures of their day and posting it to a story for all to see. If they were at a sleepover, then everyone knew it. And if you weren't invited, you definitely knew it. I'm sure there is a constant battle in young girls' heads saying, *Why is their life so much better than mine? Why was I not invited? Do I even have friends?* When I was a kid, and I was completely ditched—I didn't know about it because it wasn't shoved in my face.

I know that many other problems come with the social media craze. I know they are now comparing themselves with others enough to cause depression and much deeper emotional issues. This breaks my heart. The kids are looking for satisfaction in other people's praises, such as the number of likes they get and the uplifting comments.

So I'm not looking to get rid of it. I'm not wanting to change it. I just want the daughters of this world to know this ....

You are beautiful. You are unique. You don't need to be someone that you are not. You need to marry a boy who is obsessed with you. If you feel as if you need to send him nude pictures or he may break up with you, he is not the person for you. If he says that he will break up with you if you don't sleep with him, he is not the one for you.

The person you choose had better treat you like a princess. You cannot settle with a loser guy because you are afraid of being alone. Believe me, it is better being alone than being with "that" guy. You should have sweatpants and afro hair days. You don't always have to look social media ready. If you have a pimple, go to school anyway. If you are hurting, talk about it. Don't ever cut yourself, it just makes the pain worse. And don't ever listen to that voice that says, "Kill yourself; it will make everything better." It's a lie.

If it hurts you to look at someone's story because you will feel left out, then *don't* look at it. Unfollow such people. If there are people who cause you to make bad choices, don't follow them. Learn self-control. Don't become that person who has no life outside of social media and just becomes a vegetable on the couch. Exercise, daydream, go for a walk, be bored, get together with friends, and put your phone down. Don't judge people; it's just not nice. "Do to others what you would have them to do to you" (Luke 6:31). And lastly, you are so very loved—so, so much. God made you so special that you don't need other people to tell you so; just know it!

Father help us navigate this generation of social media. I pray you will protect children from low self-esteem and rejection. I pray you will give parents wisdom in navigating this new world of parenting and social media. I pray you will encounter our kids and help them have their own relationship with you. Father, we dedicate our children to you, and we pray you will use them to do mighty things on this earth and that they will lay every distraction aside. Thank you for your faithfulness. Amen.

3

DO UNTO OTHERS

The golden rule in the Bible says to "do to others as you would have them do to you" (Luke 6:31). A simpler way to put it is to treat people the way you want to be treated. It is an utterly simple yet profound statement. I use this verse on a daily basis to direct my steps. If I find myself nagging my kids all the time, I am reminded of this verse. Would I want to go visit my family if all they did was nag me? I never would want my kids to avoid coming home because of my behavior. Would I want to be yelled at, or would I want to be treated with kindness?

This verse comes up pretty much every day in my life. Would I want someone to help me if I were sick? If I were behind a counter working at my job, would I want someone treating me rudely? If I were a waitress, would I want customers complaining every time they came in? Would I want someone complimenting me on my super cute outfit? Would I want someone to let me know I did a good job on the sermon I'd just preached? Would I want someone to offer to help watch my children? If I love it when people help me, I want to make sure that I offer help to others. If I love it when people tell me I did well, then I want to look for ways to bless others with kind words. Not that I am living for the praises of others, but it feels good to receive words of affirmation. If I didn't like it when people are rude to me, then why would I be rude to others?

I have worked many jobs in customer service where I was treated both terribly and wonderfully. I never want to be the person who complains all the time; I want to be the person who is kind and complimentary of the service. I have some clients I always look forward to seeing because of the way they treat me. I want to make sure I treat others in the same way these special clients treat me. A negative attitude never gets you very far.

I love that, influenced by the Bible, millions refer to this as the "Golden Rule." It really can help in every area of your life. It will help in work, in parenting, and in your friendships. Would I want to be invited to go on an outing with a friend? It takes being a friend to have a friend, and you can't just wait to be invited all the time. Be the friend who reaches out. Be the parent who pursues their kids. Be the sister who makes the first call. Be the peacemaker in the family. Be the sprinkler of kindness. Would you want it to happen to you?

Jesus, thank you for wisdom. Remind me to treat others the way I want to be treated. Remind me to love the person in front of me. Jesus, thank you for teaching me your ways, for there is life in your wisdom. Father, I ask you for peace in my family. Finally, I pray that as I treat others well, it would be contagious, and love would spread to all of my relationships. Amen.

4

CHOOSE LIFE

Our lives are a product of many choices. God has given us free will to make choices as we see fit. You have the choice of where you want to live, whom you want to marry, and simpler things such as what you want to eat for dinner. Some choices have more of an effect on you than others. If you choose to eat junk every day for dinner, then after a while, the consequences of those choices will be evident on your body. The same goes for choosing TV over exercise. More dangerous decisions include choosing to party instead of college, choosing the wrong spouse, or making choices that would hurt those around us.

My oldest daughter is currently a freshman in college. She has had a few boys pursue her for relationships this year, and our conversations have often considered the characteristics of good husbands. I think choosing a quality husband is up there as one of the most important decisions you can make. You can pick someone who is handsome but has a terrible personality. I have met people who seem to make the worst choices in spouses. They keep doing it over and over, not learning from their past mistakes. I tell her to choose life in choosing a spouse—to choose someone who loves Jesus, who treats his family well, who looks as if he will be a great father, and who treats her as special.

I have seen many people make one bad decision after another, living their whole life as a product of bad choices. Their bad choices end up bringing them places that they didn't have planned for themselves. These choices even take people to homelessness, major credit card debt, loneliness, unsatisfying careers, addictions, and even suicide. The Bible says in Romans 6:23 that "the wages of sin is death; but the gift of God is eternal life through Christ Jesus our Lord." This means that the product of our bad decisions is death— not just a physical death, but a life of brokenness and not peace. The good news is the second part of the verse, which says that there is hope. Through Jesus, anything can be turned around. Any bad decision can be redeemed if we invite Jesus to transform our lives.

Today let's invite Jesus into every area of our life. Let's ask him to redeem our bad decisions and to help us in the decisions that we are making in the future. Let's ask him for help in the small decisions that affect us slowly, and let's ask for help with the big decisions that can affect us long term. Let's ask him for wisdom and to direct our steps so that we can have the fullness of life.

Jesus, come on in and saturate every part of my life. Father, forgive the choices in my past that have not been wise. Forgive my bad choices that may have affected someone else's walk. I pray that you would bestow on them a crown of beauty instead of ashes. Today I choose life. I choose to follow you instead of my flesh. I choose to ask for wisdom and guidance. I choose to honor you with my life. Father, I thank you for your mercy and grace. Amen.

5

BE THE FIRST TO FORGIVE

One of the biggest things that I have noticed causing torment in people's lives is unforgiveness. In my travels doing ministry trips, many people have opened up to me about the pain in their lives. I notice often that much of their pain results from hurts in their past. I have seen all levels of hurt healed from the simple act of forgiving their enemy.

The Bible is very clear that we give Satan access to cause torment in our lives if we entertain thoughts of unforgiveness. Second Corinthians 2:10–11 says, "Anyone you forgive, I also forgive. And what I have forgiven—if there was anything to forgive—I have forgiven in the sight of Christ for your sake, in order that Satan might not outwit us. For we are not unaware of his schemes."

In ministering, I try to be very clear that although you are forgiving, that doesn't mean that what the other person did to hurt you was okay; it just closes the door to the enemy's access into your life. I have seen some of the most horrific hurts that people have endured, but the minute they let those perpetrators go and chose to forgive them, I saw them changed, free, lifted, and many times healed either physically or mentally. The Bible is clear that walking in unforgiveness is not an option. Matthew 6:14–15 says that "if you forgive other people when they sin against you, your heavenly Father will also forgive you. But if you do not forgive others their sins, your Father will not forgive your sins."

Forgiveness is a choice, and when you let Satan, the accuser of the brethren, put lies in your head, tormenting your mind by repeating the incident over and over, soon you can't think of anything else, and it makes you crazy. Satan's number-one goal is to get you to quit in life and give up, but your job is to fight back. Your job is to wake up each day and say, "Not today, Satan." You may have to repeat it in faith for some time until you choose to forgive your enemy. You keep saying it by faith enough times that one day you will be shocked that you are no longer bothered by the lies.

When someone hurts me, I pray for them and radically bless them. The Bible says that we need to pray for our enemies and bless them. I really don't feel like it at the time, but before I know it, I am no longer hurt by their actions. I have seen this bring freedom to all levels of hurt. It releases you from the torment.

Father, I ask you to come in and forgive my enemies. Jesus, I release those that have hurt me into your hands. I go back to the very beginning of my life, and I ask you to forgive anyone that has caused pain in my life, even back then. I pray that you would release me from any pain that I have been carrying due to unforgiveness, whether it be physical pain or emotional pain. Forgive me for holding resentments toward others, and I pray that you would create in me a clean heart. Jesus, come in and have your way in me. Amen.

6

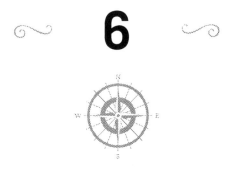

BE STILL

The high school prom was two nights ago in our little town of Petersburg. For a hairdresser, it is the busiest time of the year. Not only do we do a lot of styling on that day, but for weeks ahead of time, all the girls and guys are getting color and cut to look their best for that special day.

Through this time of craziness, I've learned the importance of protecting myself against burnout. I have been doing hair for about twenty years now, and throughout this time, I have gone through many phases of burnout. When I first started working, I was full of excitement and fire for my business. I wanted it to be hugely successful, and I wanted to make all of my clients happy. I used to worry endlessly about what everyone thought of me, and because I didn't want to let anyone down, I would stay late every night just to get everyone in. As you can imagine, it didn't take long to reach the point of burnout and exhaustion. Many times I even gave up my days off because I didn't know how to say no, and there was always one more person I just had to squeeze in.

God has been teaching me during this time some lessons about managing my life. I don't always live these lessons perfectly, but on this journey, I am learning and growing and hopefully I will have it down someday. Lately my biggest lesson is that if I am burnt out, I have nothing to give to anyone. We need to be vessels that are fully filled so that we can spill out on to everyone around us, ready to spill out Jesus to the world. If you are in the state of burnout, you have lost your hope and there is not a lot of love to share.

In the midst of all this prom craziness, I let my guard down and allowed myself to get far too busy and burnt out again. I recognized that I didn't like where I was going in my head, so I woke up early and started out on a prayer walk. I cried out to God to fill me once again with passion. I cried out to him to fill me with fresh fire. I was no good to anyone if I was walking around on empty. I needed passion and excitement that only come from an encounter from Jesus! We are not fully alive unless we are ignited on fire by Jesus. He never fails; when I cry out to him, he listens and gives me hope again.

Lesson number two is that I have to take a day of rest. In the Bible, it talks about Jesus getting away to be alone with his heavenly Father. Luke 5:16 says that Jesus often withdrew to lonely places and prayed. If Jesus did that, I'm sure it's important that we do it as well. I'm finding that many times, we have to fight for alone time. In this day and age of technology, I'm easily distracted by picking up my phone and just "checking" something really quick, and then before I know, it I'm sucked into scrolling my Facebook feed. The devil often tries to lure us into extreme busyness because he knows how to get us distracted from what really is important.

If we are fully filled with Jesus, we are unstoppable. So in order to do that, I have to learn to say no, realizing that other people's problems are not my crisis. I have to protect myself and my kids. If I am so busy helping others that I am not here for my kids, they will resent me. I have to be intentional with my time.

Most importantly, I have to put Jesus first. I have failed many times at this, but I do want to be a light to the world. I want to be fully alive and fully free, no longer bound up.

Jesus, fill us all. Help us to be still. Restore us who are burnt out, that we would feel alive again. Teach us to say no when we need to and yes when you want us to. Guide us in our coming and going. Restore unto us the joy of our salvation, and renew a right spirit within us. I pray Psalm 51:10 over me and my family. Amen.

7

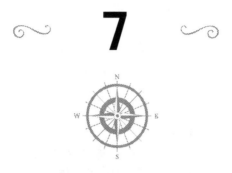

DON'T QUIT

Yesterday during my prayer walk, I started thinking about my beauty school days. I thought about some of my hardest moments in learning to be a hairdresser. There was the time my very first client came in. I immediately ran to the bathroom to throw up because I was so nervous. Another moment that stood out was the first time I did a manicure for a wedding. She was not happy with the French tips I tried to give her, so she went to my head instructor and complained about me. That happened more than once during my time there. Whenever people complained about me, I just wanted to throw in the towel and quit.

I was thinking on my walk how glad I am that I stuck it out during those hard times and didn't quit. I had a choice to make in my life; I could fight through and endure it, or I could just give up. It made me think of the many other kids out there who may have given up on their dreams because they seem too hard.

At that same school we were instructed that we always needed to act like a duck. Ducks on the surface of the water are calm and majestic looking, gliding effortlessly along the water. But what we don't see under the surface is their little legs vigorously kicking. Teachers told us that when we encounter a situation in our work, we need to keep calm and confident, while underneath working like crazy to come up with a plan to solve the crisis. I have used this many times in my life. When life gets hard and I want to quit, I just stand up tall and act like a duck. Now I know I can also ask the Holy Spirit in those times for wisdom and peace. He then fills my mind with strategies to solve my problem at hand.

But I noticed that I had a tendency to want to throw in the towel quickly when times got tough, not just in school or work but in other areas of my life as well. This I realized through my husband. He is a strong person who doesn't get frazzled by anything. He manages many businesses and apartment buildings. I always tell him he should have his own reality show because there is always something off the wall that he is trying to solve. My husband doesn't let things bother him; he just solves things one at a time. It could be chaos all around him, but he just handles it. I, on the other hand, might just want to quit our marriage or the business or just move to another town when I couldn't take the pressures of life. God knew I needed a husband who was a rock, not swayed by all types of pressures. I'm glad we persevered.

So here is my message. Don't quit. Life will be hard at times, but don't quit. School will be hard, marriage will be hard, your job will be hard, and being a parent at times will be hard. But you can do it. Don't quit the minute pressures start coming. James 1:2–3 says to be happy when you are tested in different ways because the testing of your faith produces endurance. The end result will be beautiful.

Father, give us the strength to persevere when the storms of life get tough. Help us not to quit but to press on toward our goal.

Put people in our lives to help us and to encourage us. Help us to endure and to overcome all of life's pressures. Jesus, we thank you for strengthening us and for getting us through the hardships. I thank you for making something beautiful out of our lives. Amen.

8

MOM

Someone once told me that if you help change one person's life, you not only change their life, but you may impact an entire generation. Your impacting that one life has the potential to change how that person will parent; then it trickles down, starting with that one act of selflessness.

My life is a product of someone's act of generosity. I was a kid in a bad situation; my biological mom suffered from mental illness and wasn't able to raise me. Because of that, I was moved around from home to home, some homes better than others. I was able to see my biological mom at times, but most of my young life I was in foster care.

When I was six years old, my biological mom's sister and her family came to visit in California. They then made the selfless decision to take me in. They had four kids of their own, but they chose to adopt me.

Now that I'm older and grown, I've been thinking about the

significance of that one act of kindness. Because they were able to step outside themselves, I was able to learn what family was. I was able to learn what normal was and how to grow up in a family that was safe from anger and abuse. I learned how to love, and the importance of going to church every Sunday and putting God first in my life.

I learned the joy of having a family who shares meals around the table. They shared their fun traditions with me, like pizza every Friday night for dinner and biscuits every Sunday for breakfast. Things like waking up on Christmas morning with gifts out, and sunrise service on Easter morning. They gave me the gift of travel. I sat in the backseat on road trips, and I even got to experience traveling overseas.

But the best part of my life was learning what normal was: lying outside, playing one on one basketball with my brother, having food money when I traveled for sports, and being expected to do homework. Because I learned what normal was, I was then able to pass that on to my kids. I can pass on tangible traditions like pizza on Fridays, Christmas morning presents, and going to church every Sunday. I also want to pass on the intangible traditions that I learned too, like living in a peaceful home, being kind to others, and helping people who may not be able to help themselves. I think in raising our kids, we forget how amazing it is that we pass on normal. I always want to give my kids the Disneyland experience, but the most far-reaching aspect of getting to be adopted was that I was shown what family is.

My mom could have said that four kids were too much, and that would have been understandable. She could have said that it would be too much for the other kids. But she didn't, and for that, I will always be grateful. My kids will raise their kids with those same lessons and traditions, and hopefully they will continue down, starting from one act of kindness.

Father, thank you for family. Help me pass on traditions to my kids that I grew up with, traditions like kindness and generosity. I pray that my kids will always walk with you, Jesus, and that this will pass down from generation to generation. I pray that all of my generations will be blessed. I thank you for always having your hand on my family, for watching out for us and never letting us stray too far. Thank you for your grace over us. Amen.

9

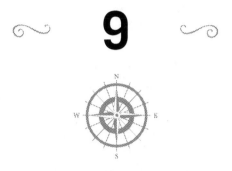

MOTHER'S DAY

A few days ago at work, I was listening to someone tell me about the Mother's Day that they had. They had a very disappointing day filled with cooking, chores, and unfulfilled expectations. It brought back memories and reminded me of a major obstacle in my life that I had overcome.

Birthdays and holidays used to be really hard for me. I would have many expectations of how the day should go—lots of spoiling and pampering, with the entire day revolving around me. At the end of the day, I was usually disappointed and frustrated that the day had not turned out how I expected. Mother's Day should be me sitting on a couch while everyone cleaned and cooked all around me. My life certainly revolved all around me.

I finally had a huge breakthrough moment in my life when I realized that I was in charge of my happiness. It isn't my husband's job or anyone else's around me. I am the one who controls whether or not I'm going to be happy. I had put lots of pressure on my husband to make sure I was living a wonderful fairy-tale life.

When I started to take ownership of my happiness, everything started to change. I started to plan fun things to do on my birthdays, like picnics or pedicure appointments. This year, I decided that on Mother's Day I wanted to take our paddleboards out on the water for a test run, and we ended up having a great time. I also did a couple of loads of dishes and cooked breakfast and lunch, but the difference was that I did it with a happy heart.

I'm not saying that my family doesn't spoil me, because they certainly do. I'm just saying that I took my expectations of them away. When I took those expectations away, I became a much happier person. I started to grow more grateful and appreciate all the little things. I realized that happiness was a choice, and I could choose to look at the negative or look at the positive. I know that when I started dwelling on what everyone was not doing, it would then open up a flood of bad thoughts about them. If I focus on the amazing parts of my family rather than dwelling on the bad qualities, then I stay in an attitude of gratitude.

From now on, I will choose to be happy, stay grateful, and appreciate even the small things. I will serve my family with a happy heart, and if I have expectations of how my day should go, then I will plan for it and communicate my feelings, not just assume that everyone can read my mind and know what I want to do. Colossians 3:15 says to let the peace of Christ rule in your hearts since as members of one body you were called to peace.

Father, help me to always have a thankful heart. Help me to become selfless and joyful. I pray that you will teach me to live a life of generosity, loving all those I come in contact with. Give me your eyes and bring healing to the areas in my heart where I have been rejected. Thank you for teaching me how to have fun. Thank you for joy. Thank you for family. I thank you for your love; I am so grateful. Amen.

10

THE GOODNESS OF GOD

The nice thing about getting older is that I can look back and see God's hand on my life. I've witnessed the goodness of God; he has rescued me, healed me, strengthened me, been a friend and a father to me, and blessed me just because he is good. A life of seeing God's hand on my life has made my faith stronger.

When I first started out on this journey, my faith was pretty weak. I told myself that I was going to spend my whole life getting to know God better, and then when I hit that magic age of thirty, I would have it all figured out. Now I'm turning forty, and I still don't have it all figured out, but my faith has grown tons. Ephesians 4:14–16 talks about us maturing and says that we will no longer be infants tossed back and forth like the waves and blown here and there by every type of teaching. It says we will grow to be mature. I do not have it all figured out yet, but through all my experiences, I have become a little more mature, and my knowledge of how good Jesus is has grown.

The first miracle of Jesus's goodness in my adult life was when we bought our first house. My faith was very minimal, but we prayed with the church that we would be able to buy a house. I was very pregnant, and we were living with my in-laws, so at the time, I felt pretty desperate. We found a house that was a small fixer-upper, but there was another couple who was also interested in the same house. That other couple had all the cash on hand to get it, and we barely had enough credit to even be considered for a loan at that point in our lives. I was fearful, thinking that we were doomed, but God in his goodness turned an impossible situation into a miracle. The homeowner chose us for that house instead of the buyers with the entire amount in cash! That started the building of my faith.

Since that time, I have seen God pull me out of a pit of depression, give my life passion, rescue us in financial crisis, do miracles in my kids' lives, miraculously provide money for mission trips, and perform many other miracles. A big one that comes to mind is when I had a mass discovered next to my uterus. The ultrasound showed that my ovary was the size of a basketball and they were worried that it might be cancerous. Once again, I cried out to God as my healer. Again, he was faithful. I went into surgery and found that this mass wasn't even my ovary at all but just a free-floating mass that was easy to remove with no trace of cancer. Not only was I healed, but God also erased my debt of $30,000 for the surgery! The only thing I could do was shed tears of thankfulness.

Looking back, I have seen him prove to me over and over how good he is and how much he loves me. When you put your life in his hands and trust him, he will take you on this faith journey where it grows and grows. I can declare in confidence that I trust him. When the doubts start to come, I speak out that I trust him! I trust that he makes all things work for good; I trust that he loves my kids and that if I place them in his hands, he will make something beautiful out of their lives as well. I can't wait to see the amazing things that he will accomplish in the years to come. The Bible says to trust in the Lord with all your heart and not to lean on your own understanding. If we acknowledge Him, then He will direct our paths (see Proverbs 3:5–6). It also says to seek first the kingdom of God, and then everything you need will be added unto you (Matthew 6:33).

Father, I thank you for all the times in my life when you were working on my behalf. Thank you for all of the miracles. Thank you for your love and kindness. I have seen you do so many amazing things in my life, and I praise you for that. Father, I ask you to make yourself real to those around us and show them your goodness and power. Amen.

11

HOUSE PROJECTS

The walls in my living room are bright orange. Once upon a time, that orange was in style, but now I'm not loving it as much. I really like the look of white walls; they look cleaner and simpler than what I have now. I know that achieving this look will take a lot of work; my ceilings are vaulted, I have many pictures already on the walls that need to come down, and I have some holes that need to be touched up before I can even get started.

The task seems daunting because I know that while I am in the process of my house makeover, the rest of the house will get messy because all of my focus is going to be on this one project. The couches are going to have to be rearranged, and I'm going to have to tape the walls and take down the curtains. But once everything is said and done, it's going to be worth it. I'm going to be glad that I made my space more inviting and more of a style that suits me.

As I went through this painting process, I thought a lot about the many situations in our lives that are similar to this experience. We can choose to be comfortable and content and have no real change happen, or we can get messy for a bit, step out, and then watch something beautiful happen on the other side. I could decide that the orange will be just fine and live with it because I don't want the hassle of the work, but I think I will jump in and see how the white looks. It may be a shade I don't like, and I may have to change it, but I will never know until I try.

For example, we may be afraid to start a new job, go to a college, buy a new house, or go to a church because we are afraid that it will be challenging. We may have to leave loved ones behind to get an education, but the result will be something great if we persevere through the hard times. However, like my painting, it may be the wrong color and we might have to tweak the process a bit. Still, God is calling us to step out of the boat and get a bit messy so that we can grow into the people he has called us to be.

My oldest daughter is starting her senior year of high school this week. It's going to be a hard transition for me to let her go next year. It would be easy for me to tell her that she can't leave and go to college and that she should just stay home with me. I think what is best for her to do is to let her go and grow. It will be hard for a time, but she will grow as a person, become more confident, learn to fail, and get some skills. I think anytime change happens, we go through some growing pains. But as a mom, I want to see her grow as a person even more than my selfish desire to keep her around. So step out, get messy, start something new, learn a new skill, go to a school, follow your heart, and don't let fear stop you. The Bible says that God has not given you a spirit of fear, but of power, love, and of a sound mind (2 Timothy 1:7 KJV).

Father, I pray that you would silence the voice of fear in my life. I pray that your voice of direction is the only voice that I hear. I pray that I never take the easy route in life but instead always do your will. Jesus, I pray for your guiding hand in every detail of my life. Amen.

12

WALLS

The other day I was visiting with a group of friends, and one of the women there made a comment that hurt my feelings. I sat there for a bit, excused myself, and then went home. I think it's funny how offended I got over one comment. I stewed on it in my head for a bit, defended myself internally for a while, and then decided the best thing for me to do was to pray.

I prayed for the person who had offended me and for myself. I asked God how my heart was and realized that I needed to choose to forgive right away to keep my heart from getting hard from unforgiveness. God showed me how I have a tendency to put up walls around my heart when people hurt me. I want to protect my heart, so I choose to not go around those people at all anymore. I was choosing to make offense my friend.

My new goal in my life is to never hold an offense. I want to be open to love people and not be afraid of people hurting me. The Bible says in Matthew (5:44) to love your enemies and to pray for those who persecute you. I think the old me would have told everyone I knew about what this friend said to me, get them to agree with me, and continue to have them tell me how great I was and how wrong this friend was. But what the Bible says is the exact opposite.

That night I went home and prayed for my friend, because that is what I'm called to do. It doesn't make sense, but it works. The next day, I was able to give her a big hug, and now I can say that I hold no bitterness in my heart toward her. What would happen if I didn't choose to forgive each person who hurt me? I believe a wall would go up around my heart; then when the next hurt came, another wall would go up. Again and again the walls would go up until the only thing I could do is stay home and become a recluse. I also believe that holding on to that hurt makes us bitter and even sick. I place all those people who have hurt me into Jesus's hands. I ask God to radically bless them, then I ask God if I have any more hurt in my heart that needs to be healed, and then I ask him to come in and heal my heart from any pain I might have. It's not easy, but it is the only way to bring freedom to your life.

Father, I place everyone who has caused me hurt and pain into your loving hands. I know that forgiving them doesn't mean what they did was right, but it releases me from the burden of carrying that pain around with me. I pray that you would bless those who have hurt me. I pray that you would bring freedom to their lives. I ask you to come and bring healing to my heart. Help me love those who are difficult to love. I pray that you would heal my mind from any negative words that have been spoken over me. Father, I thank you for being the father of restoration. Amen.

13

NEW SEASONS

School is about to start in our small town. Every time a new season in life starts, I always reevaluate how things are going and what things I need to change. Yesterday when I was looking through my scheduling book from the previous year, I found myself getting frustrated that I didn't take more time off. I noticed that I really overscheduled myself last year, and I made myself promise that this year I will take more self-care days.

I started thinking about the things that make me come alive, and I decided I need to strategically make my schedule with those things as a priority. Spending time in prayer and in the Bible is a must that always needs to come first, but other than that, I noticed that my time in exercise needed to be increased. For a while I've been adding more and more things in its place.

Other things that I need to increase in my life are piano playing, writing, and spending time with my kids and husband. I also want to add writing in a thankfulness journal. In this season, I'm wanting to change my mind-set to become more aware of the things I'm thankful for and less aware of the problem areas. I want to write every night in my journal those little things that make me feel thankful that day.

I know that we need to be intentional with our time, or else time will pass us by, and pretty soon we'll wonder where it went. My oldest daughter is a senior this year, so I know I want to make the most of these last days of her being a kid. My girls have been a blessing to raise, and I want to look back knowing I made the most out of this time with them.

I'm learning that this whole process starts in my mind. I make my mind up about the person I would like to be and go for it. I want to be a good wife, a good mom, a healthy person inside and out, and, most important, a radical Jesus follower. I've decided that I may need to wake up earlier to squeeze that workout in, stay up a little later when my daughter is finally opening up to me, and maybe say no to the cheesecake everyone else is having—but the reward far outweighs the sacrifice. I know I may fail many times, but I've made up my mind to keep pressing on toward my goals each day, one at a time.

Father, more than anything I want closeness with you. My relationship with you is my number-one priority. Help me put everything in its proper place after that. Help me to have strength and discipline to say no when I need to say no and to say yes when I need to say yes. Father, help me to have a life filled with peace. Amen.

14

JUST DO IT

The other day, I finally turned in my city sales tax for my hairdressing business. I was a few months late, and I'm sure I piled up my share of late fees. I tend to procrastinate on things when I don't want to do them. There are some things in my life that I don't enjoy, like bookkeeping, laundry, making business phone calls, and basic housekeeping. I tend to avoid them and put them off till the last possible minute. If I have to return a text because I'm afraid of letting that person down, I tend to avoid doing it until I have to. Feelings of shame come if I end up getting late fees, take a long time returning a text, or I let my housework pile up.

God is speaking to me about a better way. Usually for me, the dread of my task is much greater than the actual task itself. Yesterday I finally folded a mountain-sized pile of laundry that I had been dreading for about a week. I brought that pile into the living room and folded it while watching a movie, and before I knew it, the pile was gone.

Last week I decided to make a list of the things I needed to accomplish, with my taxes being on that list. I found real joy in crossing out the chores on that list one by one. Those taxes ended up taking me no more than an hour, so I'm pretty sure I spent way more time dreading those taxes than I spent actually doing them, and the peace that came from completing my list really was great. I also started giving myself positive self-talk. Instead of cultivating thoughts of shame, I encourage myself and give myself pep talks.

Here is my lesson: Bulldoze that list. Don't put things off until another day. Don't listen to thoughts of dread and shame. Tell yourself that you've got this. It feels better to be responsible and on task than to procrastinate and be behind. Letting things slide can have giant consequences. Growth can be painful, but we can come out stronger on the other end. Finally, as Nike says, "Just do it."

Father, help us to be kind to ourselves. I pray that you would help us take the next step in maturing. I pray that we would never have the crippling fear of what others think. Help us not to put things off till the last minute, but to confidently overcome our tasks. Put others in our lives to help us and to encourage growth. I thank you for your grace and mercy and for always being there to catch us when we fall. Amen.

15

STICK SHIFT

My oldest daughter's car has been sitting outside broke down for a couple of months. It has a manual transmission, which she figured out how to drive fairly quickly. Not very many kids in high school know how to drive a stick shift, so in her kindness, she has decided to teach her friends how to drive manual using her car. She is now on her third clutch, which she's had to purchase herself, and the car is now parked and waiting to be repaired.

As I look at this car in my driveway, I am noticing how much our lives resemble this car. If we let the wrong people take control of our car and our life, we will end up broken down. We need to stop hanging out with the wrong people, those who cause us to be "broken" or to "run funny." Are we influencing them, or are they influencing us?

Just as our car needs to be maintained, we also need to maintain our spiritual life. Some people go and go, and then suddenly break down. To maintain our car, we need to check the oil, put good gas in it, fix the parts that go out, and pay attention to the warning lights. If that car breaks down, it is useless. We will also be useless to the people around us if we are not maintaining ourselves properly. If we are not praying, reading the Word, staying connected with the right people, resting, and learning to have fun, then before long we as people will get a "check engine" light on. Those "lights" look like being easily irritated, feeling overwhelmed, getting caught up in sin, taking offense, and many other symptoms. Just like cars, we need occasional checkups to gauge how we are doing.

God is the ultimate mechanic, but first we need to make the choice to drive our car to the shop. We need to make the choice to put God first and to give our sin to him. He can fix our tormenting thoughts, free us from sin, and give us peace and joy. Going to church, reading the Word, playing worship music in the house, and praying on walks are simple ways I maintain my "car." John 15:4 says "Remain in me, as I also remain in you. No branch can bear fruit by itself; it must remain in the vine. Neither can you bear fruit unless you remain in me."

Father, you are the ultimate mechanic. As we abide in you, I pray that you would fill us with abundant peace. I pray that if things are out of order in our lives, you would nudge us in the right direction. I thank you for growth in our lives. Amen.

16

LOVE

I am going through a time right now where I am learning to love challenging people. Our greatest call in life is to learn to love everyone. About six years ago, I was going through a challenging time where we were trying to help people out but kept getting beat down and beat down. After some time, I got a text from a friend who asked if I wanted to go to a Christian conference all about love. I ended up going and started telling her my sob story about how everyone was being mean to us and how we were just trying to help people. I then asked her what we should do. She took a sec and then said something that has forever marked me. She said, "Tiffany ... you love them all."

I felt sharply convicted. I was only loving those who were easy to love. Luke 6:32–35 says,

> If you love those who love you, what credit is that
> to you? Even sinners love those who love them.

> And if you do good to those who are good to you, what credit is that to you? Even sinners do that. And if you lend to those from whom you expect repayment, what credit is that to you? Even sinners lend to sinners, expecting to be repaid in full. But love your enemies, do good to them, and lend to them without expecting to get anything back. Then your reward will be great, and you will be children of the Most High, because he is kind to the ungrateful and wicked.

Yesterday on my walk, God was speaking to me about how it was an honor to have people in your life who are hard to love. Having difficult people in our lives strengthens us; then when we go to love others, it really is a lot easier. Anyone can love the lovable, but can you love those who are hard to love? Can you love those who have just spread rumors about you? Can you love those who have wronged you? Jesus did. Jesus died on the cross while many were throwing stones at him. His words were "Forgive them, for they know not what they are doing."

Father, help us to love as Jesus does. Remind us to be kind, forgiving, and accepting of all. Help us treat people the way you would treat them. Help our minds to be full of peace, rather than filled with turmoil from overanalyzing everyone's actions. I pray that you would heal our hearts from hurtful words or actions that have caused damage. We ask you to bless our enemies. Amen.

17

TEMPERATURE

I've been thinking a lot lately about the atmosphere that I want in my home. Do I want the atmosphere to be loving or mean? Gentle or tough? Happy or sad? I want my kids to have a positive home environment full of peace and love. I want my voice to be encouraging and uplifting rather than trying to intimidate my kids.

I just returned from watching my girls play volleyball in a town close by. I noticed how much our voices can change the whole atmosphere of the game. The first night when I got to the gym, I noticed that the team was pretty down. They had lost, and I had missed the game, but as I was talking to my daughter, she said the most discouraging part was that the team started getting frustrated with each other. They started tearing each other down instead of building each other up.

I decided to be that loud cheerleader mom yelling, "Good job!" at the top of my lungs. I wanted to build up the team, to get them fired up. If one person can tear a team down by their words, then another person can build a team up by their encouraging words. The uplifting atmosphere changes everything.

I also noticed how their coach was the most encouraging coach I had ever seen. He has a gift of being firm yet kind at the same time. What a difference that makes! The kids want to please him because he has their respect.

I want to remember this concept for my home. I don't want the atmosphere to feel uncomfortable because of yelling and anger. I want it to be warm, comfortable, and full of peace and encouragement. I want to be encouraging, like the volleyball coach. If our home environment starts to get a little tense, I want to clean up my mess and fight hard to keep our home from getting chaotic. I want our words to be uplifting, and I want to gently correct if words start to tear people down.

This concept holds true in every setting: our workplace, our schools, and with our friends. We should always be in charge of the atmosphere around us, and we should be the encourager who shifts the environment. Be the person who stands out. Be the person who encourages, who doesn't talk about others behind their backs. Be a positive person in a job full of Eeyores. Then sit back and watch the temperature change around you. Watch it go from tense to calm.

Father, help us have a loving environment for our kids to grow up in. I pray that we may shift the atmosphere everywhere we go. Help us bring kindness and love to everyone we come in contact with. Father, fill our homes with a temperature of peace. Amen.

18

HAPPINESS

I grew up watching fairy tale movies, and one of my favorite things to do still is watch a good chick flick. I love it when all ends well and they live happily ever after, but rarely do the movies show what goes on five years down the road. The movies usually end with a kiss, the credits roll, and then the rest is up to your imagination. They don't show the sleepless nights when they have babies, the business struggles, or the fights over who does what chores around the house. When I was in my early twenties, I bought into the lie that the movies are real and that the happily-ever-after shouldn't require work.

I married young, at age twenty, just out of beauty school. I came into the relationship with those mind-sets brought on by the movies. I did have the happily-ever-after moment when we got married, but then the real work began. My husband moved us to Alaska so he could fulfill his dream of owning his own business. At that point I was in love with being in love, so I gladly went along with his idea. After a long winter of darkness and cold, though, I started missing the Arizona sunshine.

I started to believe a lie in my head that the only way for me to be happy again was to move back to Arizona. I gave my husband endless pressure about it until finally one day he snapped and said that we could move back. I paused and realized that I didn't really want to move; I just wanted him to say that we could so I wouldn't feel trapped. I was relying on him for my happiness. I wasn't taking care of myself by getting a hobby or getting out and being social and active. Most important, I wasn't spending time in my Bible and prayer. At that point in our marriage, all I knew was that I wasn't happy and that it was his fault.

Now, twenty years later in our marriage, we have grown a lot in our communication. I am better about communicating my needs to him and not just assuming that he should read my mind. I am better about going out hiking and walking. I have even gone on some mission trips by myself and have met some new friends who have filled a sense of adventure that I had longed for. I am better about carving time out in my day to get into my Bible. I have also picked up some hobbies like playing the piano and writing. I don't rely on my husband to make me happy, although he does. Marriage cannot be all feelings; it is waking up every day making the choice to stay in a commitment with Jesus at the center of it. I take care of me, and he takes care of him; then, when we are together, we are a strong and healthy couple.

Father, I thank you for wisdom. I thank you for your presence in my relationships and for strengthening them. I pray that you will lead me and guide me in all that I do. I pray that you would restore any wrong thinking that I have believed, either from past hurts or from lies that have been spoken to me. I'm thankful that you are the restorer of all things broken and that there is nothing impossible for you to fix. Amen.

19

BEING INTENTIONAL

Recently I was talking to a guy who had returned a few months earlier from a life-changing experience at a church retreat. This was the first time that he had really encountered God, and it was completely life-changing for him. He was on fire for God when he came home, but over time, the fire that had started at that retreat was slowly growing dim. He began to get sucked back into life as usual, full of friends, video games, and the pursuit of work. He didn't find a local church to get plugged into, and he stopped reading the Bible. It didn't take long for him to grow spiritually dry.

I've noticed that this is a huge problem for Christians who come out of Bible schools, mission programs, or even Christian speaking events. They get inspired and excited about the things of God—until they get home and stop feeding that flame. Slowly then that flame will start to flicker and finally go out.

The good news is that if your fire burns out, there is still hope. Your flame can be relit. The Bible says to draw near to him, and he will draw near to you. We need to stop the things that are stealing our time from reading the Word. When I was at my lowest point in life, I made a decision that I had to either run after God with everything I had in me or else be buried in depression. I decided that I needed to be intentional with my life. I made a choice to read the Word every day, pray every day, and write in my prayer journal. That was all I knew to draw near to God. I felt God near when I started having my quiet times with my worship music on. I just took the first step to draw near to God, and then he continually drew near to me.

We have to be intentional about our time. I'm finding that if we don't plan our time, it can easily get stolen from us. We need to schedule going to church and being in fellowship with others. We need to make the decision to read the Word or decide to shut off Facebook a little sooner in the evening.

I have to schedule out my time to exercise and grocery shop and also schedule time with my husband and family. If I leave it to chance, I may get through a whole week not having spent any quality time with my husband or even cracked open my Bible once. If my husband and I have a busy week and neglect any quality time, then we both start feeling like roommates instead of husband and wife.

Take that first step. Resist the fear of going to a church. We need each other. Go to a conference to have more "gasoline" dumped on you. Get that flame burning again. Pray in the spirit. Read books of revivalists around the world. Put that worship music on. Journal. Before long, that flicker inside you will grow into a raging fire.

Father, we ask you for fire again. I pray that you would revive us. If we have grown cold, I pray that you would stir us up. I pray that we would become passionate again. Come and pour out the Holy Spirit on us; we need a touch from you. Father, make us hungry again, we need your presence. Amen.

20

POTTY TRAINING

When my girls were babies, I went through a season where the only things I thought about were potty training and teaching them to sleep through the night. From the time my oldest daughter arrived, she had her days and her nights mixed up. I was a young mom who had no tricks up her sleeve, so I just decided to conform to her ways. Every night I rented some movies and stayed up with her. Some nights we drove around, desperate to calm her if she was fussy. Some nights I was exhausted, but I just couldn't seem to figure out how to switch her sleeping patterns.

When my second daughter came along, the only prayer I had for her life was that she would be a good sleeper. God had mercy on me, and she was an amazing night sleeper, but she had colic every evening from about six o'clock until nine. I figured out that the only thing that would calm her was baths. I would bathe her for hours each night just to keep her calm. Don't get me wrong; my girls were adorable and sweet, but there were days when I dreamed of naps and long vacations.

The next stage that came along was potty training. I was consumed with trying to figure this out. If I could just get them to sleep through the night and be potty trained, I was succeeding at motherhood. But once again, my girls were being stubborn about the whole process of potty training. I literally thought that my daughter was never going to be potty trained and that she would walk down the aisle to meet her husband in a diaper. I asked everyone I knew their advice, and they freely gave me their tips. I tried them, but in my head, this was an enormous problem.

One day I was talking to my mom, and she said, "You know, Tiffany, you don't see kids in middle school wearing diapers. She will get through this." I then decided that this really wasn't a crisis—that this too would pass.

Sure enough, it did pass. My girls are now seventeen, fifteen, and ten. They are all very much potty trained. When I was thinking about this the other day, I realized that a lot of times we magnify the problem in front of us instead of thinking, "Is this really going to be a problem five or ten years down the road?" I never even think about the stress of potty training anymore; we are now moving on to issues like peer pressure and college. These too shall pass.

Hold on to Jesus. Don't let go. Don't worry about anything. Pray about everything. Enjoy every moment.

Father, I cast all of my worries onto you! Take all of my care and fear, and fill me with joy. I thank you for all of the blessings around me. I thank you that you are in control of my life and that you are making something beautiful out of it. I thank you for your hand on every member of my family. I pray that you would saturate us with your presence so that we would feel nothing but peace and hope. Thank you, Jesus. Amen.

21

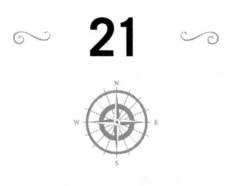

VOLLEYBALL

"Disappointments are inevitable; discouragement is a choice." I saw that quote by Charles Stanley the other day, and it made me think about my two oldest daughters, who are playing high school volleyball. We had just spent the weekend watching match after match, and I couldn't help but notice the different expressions on all of the players. I noticed that when the girls were doing well, they were pumped up and excited, but I also noticed that when some of the girls started messing up, they would get mad at themselves and others. Some got so frustrated that they were almost in tears, ready to be subbed out.

On the other hand, I noticed a few who were making mistakes but kept their heads in the game and continued having good attitudes. Those were the kids who impressed me. Despite their frustration, they were choosing not to become discouraged.

This brought back memories of when I played basketball in high school. Back then, I thought sports were everything. I spent much of my free time playing, and at the time I thought basketball was my whole world. I really was crushed when I made mistakes and had to get subbed out.

I wish I could go back and whisper in my younger self's ear that discouragement was a choice. I would tell myself not to put so much pressure on myself but instead to just have fun. I would also encourage myself to remember that in five years, my biggest problem wouldn't be the team I didn't join or the playing time I didn't get. I would say, "Keep your head up. Don't sulk when you make mistakes, and especially don't blame mistakes on your teammates." If we can learn these lessons in sports, they will carry into the rest of our lives.

There will be times when you will have disappointments. There may be disappointments in your job or with your kids, financial setbacks, or low points in your health. Will you then just hang your head and quit? Will you yell and blame those around you? Or will you keep fighting?

We need to stay calm in the storm. The enemy roams around like a roaring lion, seeking whom he will devour. Don't let that be us. Let us be warriors, strong and mighty in battle.

Father, walk with us through the fire the way you did with Shadrach, Meshach, and Abednego. I pray that you would walk with us through the fires and storms of our lives. I pray that you would shut the mouths of lions that are trying to take us out. Father, teach us how to have a godly character. Fill us up with so much of your love that it spills onto all those around us. Thank you, Father, for fighting our battles. Amen.

22

JUDGE NOT

While watching volleyball this weekend, I was reminded how easy it is to judge others. When watching sports, it's easy to take cheap shots at people because we assume they will never hear us. When other people aren't around, it's so easy to point out their flaws. I think sometimes we judge others to make us feel better about ourselves.

I found myself needing to repent this morning. The Bible tells us in Luke 6:37, "Do not judge, and you will not be judged. Do not condemn, and you will not be condemned. Forgive, and you will be forgiven." Basically, it says that if we judge others, we also will be judged.

This also brought to mind the story in the Bible about the woman caught in adultery (see John 8:1–11). In this story, the teachers of the law and the Pharisees have brought in a woman caught in adultery, and they want to stone her. Jesus then stops them and says, "Let any of you who is without sin be the first to throw a stone at her" (verse 7). After he says this, the accusers walk away. Jesus then says, in effect, "I don't condemn you ... go and leave your life of sin." Jesus is saying that we all have flaws, so don't point out other people's. Who on this earth is perfect?

I'm finding that it's easy in this day and age to pick people apart on social media. Everyone is wanting to be validated by posting selfies on Instagram. We want lots of likes and comments on how great we look. But in this quest for validation, it's easy to judge other people's photos and tear down others to build our own self-esteem.

I will try my best not to make hurtful remarks about others. When those around me are pointing fingers, I will do my best to refrain and instead choose to speak life into people. I want to build them up rather than tear them down. I will try to put myself in their shoes for a moment. From this day forward, I will do my best to live by the Golden Rule: to do unto others what I would want them to do unto me (see Luke 6:31).

Jesus, I pray that you would help me love those around me. I pray that you would guard my mouth from saying hurtful words toward others. I pray that my words would build up and encourage those around me. Father, forgive me if I have used my mouth to cause harm. Amen.

23

KIDS

"Train up a child in the way that they should go, and when they are old, they will not depart from it" (lightly paraphrasing Proverbs 22:6 KJV). Although the Bible clearly offers this wisdom, I see the trend to let kids choose whether or not they would like to attend church.

I'm passionate about training our children and making going to church a habit. When I was young, my parents took us to church every Sunday; it's just what we did. I then graduated and went off to college, so when Sunday came around, I knew that it was church day. I then had to make the decision if I was going to make my faith my own. I decided that it wasn't just my parents' faith, but that I needed to have my own relationship with God. If we choose not to go to church because we've somehow been offended in the church, because we're tired on Sundays, or because we just can't find a church we like, then we are doing our children a huge disservice.

If we don't make God a priority in our lives, why would we

think our children will choose any different? Studies show that kids who grow up in homes with parents who smoke are more likely to be smokers themselves. The fact is that our biggest testimony is how we live; the kids follow our example. I want my kids to become churchgoing world changers. When they leave my home, my prayer for them is to find a church where they can continue to grow in their faith and eventually raise their kids in the church.

Are we doing our best as parents to represent Christ to them? I want to model behavior that they can follow. If I'm kind, generous, caring for the poor, not quick to be offended, and putting God first in my life, then I'm modeling behavior that I would love to pass on. Being a full-time working mom, I understand more than anyone the struggle to find balance in life. It would be very easy to take a Sunday off to just be lazy or catch up on chores, but my duty as a mom is to help form habits in my children.

I've always been told that if we do anything for thirty days, then it forms a habit. I want to do better than that; I want their life to be a habit of goodness. I want them to know the presence of God and the value of following Jesus, and I want them to gather with others to worship him together in unity. So let's change the trend. Let's go to church and be examples to our family.

Jesus, I pray that my kids will grow to be disciples. I pray that we will always choose to run after you. I pray that my children will find a body of believers to help them grow in their faith. Heal their hearts from any area where they have been hurt by other believers. I pray that you will increase my hunger for you, Jesus, and that that passion will spill onto and influence the next generation. Jesus, set my family on fire for you. Amen.

24

I TRUST YOU

My husband and I recently bought a house about a block away that we decided to remodel and sell. My husband spent a year ripping out carpets, buying new cabinets, redoing walls, and repairing the foundation. He had an employee do a lot of the work, but that meant a lot of money was going out on this project before any money was coming in. The house ended up taking way longer than expected which made us go a bit over budget.

Then when the time finally came where we could put the house on the market, the waiting game began. We were hoping that the day we put the house up for sale, it would suddenly be snatched up. I started praying that it would sell and walking by it every day while thanking God for bringing along the right buyer for that little house. Sure enough, before long we had a breakthrough, and that house sold. Whenever I got nervous that the house wouldn't sell, I would declare out loud, "God, I trust you."

I've come to know that God is my provider—no one else but

him. The Bible says that my God will supply all of my needs, and I trust him now. I've seen him faithful to us so many times.

Two years ago, I had a health scare that racked up a bill of about thirty thousand dollars, and I needed to be able to pay for the surgery. I started to fight that battle with worship, and whenever thoughts of fear crept in, I declared, "No, I trust you, Jesus." We can't entertain those thoughts of doubt. Joyce Meyer talks about how the battlefield is in the mind. We have to take control of our own thought life. The enemy tries to prompt thoughts of all kinds of doubt, discouragement, fear, unbelief, shame, comparison, and self-doubt. The problem is that we agree with those thoughts instead of speaking what the Bible says about our situation. "My God will supply all of my needs." "By his stripes I am healed." These need to be the words spoken out of our mouths. I had a massive breakthrough in my life when that entire bill ended up being paid for by the hospital. I was in constant declaration that my God was going to supply all of my needs, and he followed through on that promise. I think about that experience often and thank God for his faithfulness.

What are those lies that are being spoken to you? Do you have thoughts of discouragement, hopelessness, and fear? Remind yourself that he is intimately close even when he feels far away. He is just waiting for you to receive him and trust him with your life. Let God be your Father. Would you place your life in his hands today?

Father, I place my life into your hands, and I trust you with it. I know that you will make something beautiful out of my life. I thank you, Jesus, for supplying all of my needs. I pray that the peace that only comes from you will take over my thought life. I praise you for being in control of my life. Amen.

25

LAWNMOWER

I was cutting a client's hair today, and she told me about a term she heard on the radio called lawnmower parenting. I immediately googled it, and this is what came up: "a parent that will intervene or 'mow down' any obstacle that stands in the way of them saving their child from any problem, inconvenience, or discomfort."

When I heard this, it brought me back to the previous week when I was watching my girls play volleyball. They were having a particularly hard week losing games; their play was off, and they were feeling frustrated that other teammates would take their positions. As a mom, it was hard to see them hurting, and inside I really wanted to make everything easy and perfect for them.

I love it when everything is going smoothly for my kids, but deep down, I know that the trials they go through build character. The Bible tells us in James to be happy when we are tested in different ways. It says that such testing of our faith produces endurance. Endure until your testing is over, and then you will be mature and complete. I think the problem with this lawnmower parenting is that if we make everything perfect for our children, they will be lacking the maturity that they need to solve problems for themselves or get over disappointments in the future. If their lives are free of struggles while they are in our homes, will they be able to deal with the struggles of living in a real world where they might lose their job, or not get the promotion that they are hoping for?

It is so tempting to fight for our kids. I've seen kids who can't call and make appointments because they are scared to ask adults for things. We as parents swoop in to save the day and make that call, fight for our kid's grade, or even complain when they are not on the right team. I've even seen kids go off to college and not get their hair cut the entire time because they aren't bold enough to make an appointment on their own. Our kids need to learn to have their own voice and not rely on ours.

I've decided that my role as a parent isn't to make my kids' lives perfect but to give them the skills they need to make it on their own and to give them the love and comfort to get them through the hard times. I want them to learn to cry out to God when they are hurting. I explained to my girls the value of learning to ask yourself this question: "Is this trial really going to matter in five years?" I went through many of the same struggles when I was in high school, and I don't ever think about them now unless I am reflecting on how I can learn from them. I want my kids to be mature and full of character, not kids who are unsatisfied unless they are the best at everything.

Father, bless my children. Help them grow to be mighty warriors for you: perfectly mature and full of character. Give them strength, and draw many people to come beside them to help encourage them in their faith. Father, guard my mouth and actions from fighting the battles that they need to face on their own. Give my children the wisdom to make godly decisions. I pray that you would always guide their steps. Thank you, Jesus, for the amazing journey of raising kids. Amen.

26

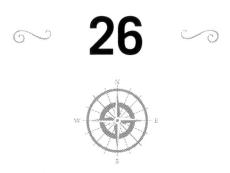

PERSONALITIES

I feel it's important to know yourself well and what you need to stay recharged. If you are introverted and never have time to recharge, doing the things that truly bring you rest, you will get burned out pretty easily. If you are an extrovert and are never allowed to visit people, you may get a bit stir-crazy over time.

My family and I were joking around last night about this. My oldest daughter, Trinity, and my husband are exactly the same; my middle daughter, Allie, and I are a lot alike, and my youngest daughter is somewhere in the middle. Whenever we go on vacation, my husband and Trinity have to look up everyone they know in the area and make plans to visit with each one. Allie and I think that a vacation on the beach visiting no one is the most relaxing way to travel.

We have many differences; my husband and daughter have always been able to visit guests until well into the night, while I have always needed ample downtime. It has been a challenge in our marriage to communicate what each other's needs are, but it has also helped me grow as a person being married to someone who continually pulls me out of my shell. I have gone on outings with him, not really wanting to go but ending up really enjoying myself. On the contrary, I have had to pull him in at times to have quiet quality family time. My husband and I use our differences to make us more well-rounded people.

I have spent many years wishing that I were bolder and more outgoing. We have to be careful not to compare ourselves with others, wishing we were more like someone else. God has made us just how he intended. There was no mistake. I think it's beautiful how in my family, we have the differences in our kids as well as in the adults. The kids have had to learn to be understanding with one another, respecting each other's wishes. I think the discomfort it may cause is good as well. It allows them to make good teams working together, pushing each other yet being understanding when the other people have needs that need to be met. On some of our trips we visit everyone, and on other trips we rest and enjoy each other. Communication and compromise need to be core values in every home.

Father, thank you that we are each uniquely and wonderfully made. I pray that you would bless our family with peace in our homes, that we would be understanding with one another and work together as a team. Thank you for the gift of family, and I pray that you would make yourself real to each member of my family so that they are confident in who you made them. My kids are destined for greatness, and no weapon formed against them will prosper. We all have a God-given destiny, so we never need to compare ourselves with others. Amen.

27

PRAYING FOR OUR KIDS

As a parent, I feel my single most important task is to pray for my kids—not just a once a week general prayer but bathing my children in prayer daily. As a parent, I have had my ups and downs during different seasons in raising my children, but one thing I have been consistent with is praying for them.

I pray over every area of my kids' lives. At times during school when I felt they were starting to have questionable friendships, I prayed that God would take away the bad influences and give them friends who would encourage them. When they needed to learn a lesson but they were having a hard time listening to me, I would ask God to teach them. The Bible gives a wonderful promise: "All your children will be taught by the Lord, and great will be their peace" (Isaiah 54:13). That is a promise that we can pray over them.

The Bible says in Matthew 9:38 to "ask the Lord of the harvest, therefore, to send out workers into his harvest field." I pray that verse regularly over my children. I ask Jesus to put people into my children's path to encourage them, to teach them, and to help them grow.

Praying the Word over our children is the most powerful way to pray for them. Oftentimes I will write their names in my journal and write underneath their names all the different areas in their lives like school, friendships, their relationship with God, sports, their future spouses, and their future. I notice at times if they are struggling in any one of those areas, and I ask God for wisdom in parenting them. I have seen God do mighty works for my kids. I have seen him shift friendships, give them favor, help them overcome fear, give them direction, and much more. God is faithful, that's for sure.

Every night at bedtime, we pray that they would have peace and that God would camp his angels around them. In the morning, I may pray that their minds would be protected from anything that they would hear or learn at school that doesn't line up with the Word of God. I pray protection over them from sickness or injury.

Praying for our children is a habit that is very necessary in this day and age. They can't just be left to let the devil have his way in their lives. They need to be covered and protected by praying that "no weapon formed against them will prevail" (Isaiah 54:17).

Father, thank you for the gift of children. They are a blessing. Father, you know my kids better than I do, so I pray that your hand would be in every area of their lives. I pray that you would radically pursue my kids and that they would reach the fullness of what you have for them. I speak greatness and destiny over my kids, that you would raise them up to be leaders and have lots of influence in their school. I break off the power of the enemy and say that he can't have my children. They are covered by the blood of Jesus. (You will steal and disrupt no more!) Thank you, Jesus, for leading them, protecting them, and guiding them. Thank you that my kids are surrounded by godly friends; I pray that you would break off any influence that isn't pleasing to you. I pray that my kids would be unashamed of you and that they would run after you with their whole hearts. I pray that you would bless each of them with a godly spouse who values them. I pray that you would camp your angels around my kids and protect them from sickness and injury. I thank you for the favor my kids have and that you are always working on their behalf! You are an amazing father. Amen.

28

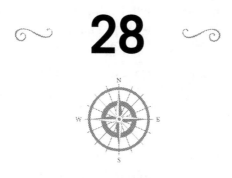

SPOUSES

My oldest daughter recently went through her first high school breakup. This has opened up a huge discussion in our house about qualities in future spouses that they are looking for. It has also caused us to take a trip down memory lane and talk about our past relationships and what we have learned from them to help the kids learn how to pick a future spouse.

I met my husband in college, and he was an instant best friend. We were comfortable together and always had a lot of fun. I knew his character was good; he was kind and thoughtful, the person who rescued people all the time. He went to church, and he treated his mom with respect. I knew that whoever married him would be spoiled.

His character is finally what drew me to him. I tell my girls that character has to be the way we choose our spouses. We cannot choose our significant other on looks alone. I also tell each of my girls to choose a guy who is almost obsessed with her. I have never worried in my twenty years of marriage if my husband was going to cheat on me because he is obvious about his love.

It's hard not to notice the many failed relationships all around us. Some people feel that their spouse no longer makes them happy, or they are no longer attracted to one another. I do know that relationships take a ton of work. My husband and I are opposites; he is a dreamer, a risk-taker, and an outgoing extrovert, while I on the other hand am practical, more of an introvert, and not a risk-taker. We have had to learn to communicate, trust each other, push each other, and forgive.

I decided that I never want to be the person who holds back my husband from his dreams, so I have let him take the risks and buy the businesses that are on his heart. I came to the conclusion that if we lost everything tomorrow, it really would be okay, and we would still have our family. We might have to move to a different location, but we would still be with our girls, playing card games at night.

I came into our relationship with some baggage that I needed to get rid of. I would shut down when we got in an argument and not talk to him for a week. He finally said that this was not the way we were going to deal with conflict. I started to open up, not go to bed angry, and take the initiative to say sorry. Admitting I am wrong is something that I used to struggle with, but now I fight to keep the peace. The Bible tells us that when there is strife in the house, the devil is free to do his work. That's why we do our best to fight to keep the peace. We try always to work as a team and communicate. We admit when we are wrong, go on date nights, and support each other's dreams.

My advice is, if you need counseling, go. Going and getting help doesn't mean you failed; it just means that you value your relationship enough to work on it. Don't quit the minute things get hard, the way I once tended to do. Marriage is something you don't just quit; you work together to get rid of each one's old baggage.

Together you need to move toward God, who has to be the center of any relationship. Pray together, go to church together, and read your Bible together.

Father, help us choose the spouse that is best for us. I pray that they would be godly and devoted. Highlight the person who is best, and keep away any who are causing me to stumble. For those who are already married, I pray for peaceful homes. Help us see our spouses the way you see them, and help us work as a team to reach our full potential in Christ. Help us learn to love and value one another. Jesus, have your way in our homes. Amen.

29

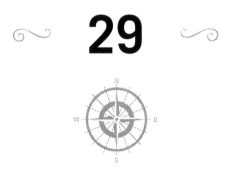

COMPARISON

On my walk today, I was thinking about my life and all the times I have wished I was more like other people. In school, I wished I was more like the girls with expensive clothes or who played better than I did in sports. As I got older, it turned into wishing I had a nicer house or that I was thinner or more outgoing. When I saw people who were more outgoing than I was, I wondered why everyone was so drawn to them and not to me. There were many days when I was left to wonder what was wrong with me.

Now that I'm a parent, it breaks my heart to see kids compare themselves with others. I see all the pressures that they carry as they try to make the team or to have a boyfriend and keep him around. I see kids taking selfies and posting them, seeking the validation of everyone telling them how beautiful they are.

As a mom, I never want my girls to compare themselves with others. I see great beauty in them just as they are. I see their kind hearts and their beautiful faces. I see their talent and their character.

I see them as vibrant and thankful. I could go on and on about how much I love them and the greatness I see in them. They are all very different but equally amazing. They all make our family well rounded.

From my time being a mom, I can start to see God's heart for us. I hear him saying "Why would you compare yourself with anyone else when you are amazing and perfectly made? Why would you spend your life trying to be someone else when you are so unique? If you could only see yourself as I see you and how you shine, why would you spend your life trying to be someone else?"

Lay down that burden and the pressure you are carrying, and give them to Jesus. See yourself with new eyes. See the good in yourself. See your talents, and stop looking at why your talent isn't like other people's. Stop looking at other people's social media accounts and wondering why they are so much more beautiful than you. You are beautiful. It's possible to acknowledge someone else's beauty without taking away from your own. Don't strive to be someone else; instead, be the best you can be. You cannot possibly carry all that pressure; you may explode.

Jesus, help. These kids need you. They need you to be real to them. They need to know how you see them and how beautifully they are made. We need our differences to grow. We pray that they would stop listening to the voices that say that they are not enough or that they aren't beautiful. Show them the little ways that they are amazing this week! I pray that you would take every burden that they are carrying and replace them all with incredible joy. Thank you for being an awesome Father who cares so much. Amen.

30

GOOD SAMARITAN

Today as I was headed to my bank to make a deposit, I saw a lady outside with bags walking in the pouring rain, heading into the bank I was going to. I knew her as someone who had a somewhat challenging personality. The thought immediately came, *Oh no, she's probably going to ask for a ride.* Sure enough, I go inside the bank, and the first thing out of her mouth is a request for me to give her a ride up the hill to her house.

That's when the story of the Good Samaritan pops into my head. In the gospel of Luke, Jesus tells a story about a traveler who is stripped of his clothing and left half beaten on the side of the road. First a priest and then a Levite walk by, who both avoid the man. Finally, a Samaritan comes upon the traveler on the road and offers help. Jews and Samaritans despise each other, but still the Samaritan helps the traveler.

I never want to be the person who walks right on by the person who needs help, I want to be the one who helps a neighbor in need.

So when this lady asked me for a ride, I got over myself and said yes because though people can be challenging, my goal on this earth is to become more and more like Christ. Jesus would stop for the one in need. He would love his enemies; he wouldn't judge challenging people.

We never know the struggles that other people are going through. I tell my girls all the time that hurt people hurt others. If people are difficult to be around, it helps to look at them through different eyes. They are most likely struggling. Most bullies at school are getting bullied themselves somehow. If we can see them with the eyes of compassion and show them love and kindness, it could begin to soften any hardened heart. The Bible tells us to love our enemies and to pray for those who persecute us. It helps to pray and ask God how he sees the person to get insight into why a person might be the way they are.

Father, help me see those around me in need. Soften my heart, and help me love those around me, even the challenging people. Help me always to stop for anyone in trouble, and give me the boldness to pray for anyone in need. I pray that I would always love my enemies, and forgive me for the times I have not loved well. Forgive me for the times I have been selfish and self-centered. May I always be growing to become more and more like you. Guard my mouth from judging others, so that my lips are only for praising you. Amen.

31

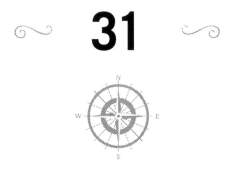

WHATEVER YOU DO

From my youngest days, I've had the desire to be a hairdresser. Whenever I visited a salon, I always thought that the hairdressers seemed utterly stylish. It was set in my mind that after graduation that was what I would do. Years went by, and I decided that I would go to a university instead, but while I was there, I never lost that desire to do hair. I just didn't want to miss out on any experience. I wanted to do college and beauty school.

After doing a year of college at Grand Canyon University, I didn't want to keep spending money when I knew that ultimately hair school was where I wanted to be. I hadn't officially made up my mind to pursue hair school until I went to bed the night before I was supposed to fly back to Arizona for college. I couldn't sleep that whole night. I couldn't shake the thought of beauty school. I felt such an urgency to go. Looking back, I know now that the urgency I felt was the Lord's leading. Many times, he leads us by the desires of our heart.

The next morning I went downstairs and told my parents that I would not be continuing college; I had a change of plans. Surprisingly, they went along with it. I finished that program and then moved back home to pursue my dream of being a hairdresser.

The hardest part of being a hairdresser is the struggle in dealing with people. I wanted to serve God with my whole heart, but the struggle not to gossip was always there. It's in the air of the hair world. I struggled so much with the gossiping that I eventually gave up hairdressing for a time. Then a massive God encounter changed all my priorities. At that moment, God became so real to me that I had to go home and get rid of anything in my life that wasn't godly. I quit my job because I felt that it was becoming petty and ungodly in my life. I wanted to give my entire life to glorify God. It says in 1 Corinthians 10:31, "Whether you eat or drink or whatever you do, do all to the glory of God." I took that verse to heart.

I then realized that there was a way that I could cut hair and not be a part of the gossip scene, and I could even use my job for good. I could counsel, encourage, and pray for my clients. I started working again, but this time, I decided to use my job to further the kingdom.

I feel that many people are being used for ministry in the workplace. Not everyone will go into a church service, but we can meet people where they are. My husband is in the rental business, and many times he is praying for people going through tough times or even offering housing to homeless people who need it. We can be a light in any profession out there. We can shine our character, and it will have an impact on those we encounter.

Not everyone is called to preach or to go to Africa, but we are all called to go into the world to share the gospel. Your Africa may be a restaurant where you are a waitress. But whatever you do, do it all for the glory of God.

Father, thank you for leading us and guiding us. I pray that you would guide us all our lives. Help us have boldness to share the gospel and to be a light to everyone around us. I pray that we would always learn to listen to your leading and guidance, and that we would never try and do this life on our own without looking to you in everything. Father, I pray that we all would have more encounters with you that are life changing. We worship you for all that you have already done and are going to do in our lives. Amen.

32

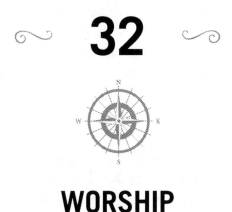

WORSHIP

Every Sunday, my husband gives the message on offering at our church. He spends time praying and perusing the Word to hear God on what to talk on, but more often than not, he gets his message during worship right before he gets up to talk. Last Sunday he talked about the importance of spending time in worship. It's important to incorporate worship into our everyday life, not just at church on Sundays.

I like to start my day in worship. Worship looks different to everyone, but in my life, I love to plug my headphones into the computer and sing along to popular worship songs. Many times, my family wakes up to me singing loudly and usually off-key. The Bible says to make a joyful noise, right? I also love to put on my headphones and go for walks where I pray and worship. For me, walking keeps me from getting distracted by all the projects that need to get done around my house.

The Bible says to enter his gates with thanksgiving in our hearts and to enter his courts with praise. When I take the time to put the worship music on while driving or pounding away on my keyboard at home, most times his presence feels tangible, and I begin to hear what he is saying to me.

Sometimes I just feel peace and joy. When that peace and joy come, then fear, anxiety, worry, depression, and all else that is coming against me begins to fade away. That's why it's so important to spend time focusing on Jesus and less time focusing on our problems. Our problems get magnified when we focus on them, but when we spend time worshipping and focusing on Jesus, we rise above our problems.

I like to keep the worship music going in my house all the time. Have you ever been in a room that is playing music that is really inappropriate, and it starts to make you feel agitated? I notice that stuff all the time. If my kids are playing songs that are not godly, I start getting really irritable. My youngest daughter picks this up as well, and she has even turned on the worship music in our home if my husband and I get into a disagreement. She also plays worship music every night as she goes to sleep because she notices that no fear arises when that music is playing. I want my house to be full of peace and God's presence, so every day I have that music playing all day, even when nobody is home.

When I went through the season in my life where I was dealing with my health and eventually needed a hysterectomy, the worship music got me through. I spent most mornings singing the song miracles by Jesus Culture. Let's make our homes worship homes so that when people come to visit, they sense the difference. Let's start our day with Jesus and getting built up so we can face the day ahead of us.

Father, I thank you for worship. Help me remember to fill my home with praise. I am thankful for what you are doing in my life and through my life. I pray that your presence would fill my home so that all who walk in would experience your peace and your joy. I pray that my kids would learn to hear your voice and not a stranger's. Thank you for teaching us and guiding us every day. We worship you. Amen.

33

EVERYTHING MUST GO

Thanksgiving was a week ago, and that has got me thinking about my relationship with food and how that relates to our lives. Years ago after my kids were born, I had made up my mind that I was going to lose the eighty or more pounds that I had gained during pregnancy. I told myself that I wanted to be a mom that they were proud of. I had turned into a person I wasn't proud of, who basically spent much of the day on the couch. My "why" for losing my weight was my kids. At that moment, I decided that everything must go. Anything that didn't benefit me somehow was eliminated from my diet, and before I knew it, I had reached my goal weight. I felt light and free, without all that extra weight dragging me down.

Years went by where I was eating in a healthy way, but every once in a while I would sneak some sugar into my diet to see how it affected my weight. At first nothing changed, so I added a little more and then a bit more of my favorite foods. Before long, the weight started slowly creeping back on, a little here and a little there, until before long I was back to the same weight that I had started with. I even tried to convince myself that I didn't want to be healthy anymore and that items like fast food pizza and burgers were impossible to give up.

I can't help but think about how this battle with food is related to our spiritual walk. Many of us have an amazing encounter with God and then go home and get rid of anything in our lives that's holding us back from growing in our faith. I remember going to youth camps as a kid and then at home burning all of my music that was ungodly. Some people may remove toxic friendships, others may burn up their porn, and some may make a commitment to stay away from the bars. Everyone has different areas that they have struggled with.

We surround ourselves with the Christian community and spend time in the Bible, and soon we are growing into Christ-followers who are full of freedom and joy. But as we go along in life, the devil tries to sneak our old patterns back into our lives little by little. We try to convince ourselves that it's okay to watch that inappropriate movie or start listening to music that is full of swearing. We even convince ourselves that skipping our Bible time won't hurt us. A little bit won't hurt us. But the problem is that this sin starts to desensitize us, and before long we're back to our old self, looking nothing like the on-fire, world-changer Christian we told God that we wanted to become. We start to feel guilty around the people who are running after God, so we start to avoid those people and church altogether.

Like my relationship with food, there is always that opportunity to recommit ourselves. Starting fresh is an amazing feeling. God is always there to wash us, transform us, and rekindle the flame that once burned brightly. After Thanksgiving, I decided that I didn't like the way I felt when I ate the pie and all the breaded food. I eliminated all the food that was bogging me down, and I feel amazingly energized again.

The devil will lie by asking, *Why even try to live the godly life?* We start to agree with him because we do fail over and over again. That's the time to tell the devil to shut up and to stop believing those lies. Jesus is always there with open arms. When you spend time with him, all those chains start to fall off once again, and before long, you are walking in freedom and victory once again.

So get up! It's time to start living again! Don't give up, but keep running! The Bible says in Deuteronomy 31:6, "Be strong and courageous. Do not be afraid or terrified because of them, for the Lord your God goes with you; he will never leave you nor forsake you."

Father, I recommit my heart to you. I ask you to forgive all of my baggage that I have let back into my life. I ask you to relight that flame inside me that once burned so brightly. I ask you to burn up any of the negative thoughts that are plaguing my mind right now and replace those thoughts with truth. I pray that you would put people in my path to help me grow and to encourage me in my faith. I thank you for always being there with open arms. Amen.

34

FEAR OF MAN

Who are these imaginary people that we are trying to impress? Ever since I was a young girl, I always had the dream of becoming a hairdresser. It wasn't the typical route of going to college, graduating, and then on to get a job. I worried constantly about what my life looked like to other people and whether they were going to be proud of me. I often feel that this fear of man and what others think of us holds us back from going after our dreams.

The Bible says (Colossians 3:2) that we need to set our eyes on things above and not on earthly things. This means to go after the dream that God has placed inside each of us and to run after that dream with our whole heart, not looking to the right or to the left to see what others may think of us. Many times when we are going after things to build the kingdom of God or grow in our faith, the enemy will put people in our path to sway us from doing what we are called to do. First Corinthians 16:13 says to be on guard; stand firm in the faith, and be both courageous and strong.

We need to pray and ask God to reveal to us those plans he has for us, then start running after all that he as for you. About five years ago, I had heard God speak to me about going on a mission trip to Haiti. I ended up applying to the mission program but didn't hear back from them for three months. One day I was driving in my car and thanking God for always taking care of me and protecting me from making any mistakes. I felt that since I hadn't heard back from this program, I may have missed hearing God correctly, and I was just lovingly thanking God for always having my back.

When I got home, I immediately looked at my email, and sure enough, there was a message accepting me and my girls into the mission program. The presence of God just fell on me at that moment, and when I was asked where we hoped to go, I quickly answered Haiti. I felt God so much at that moment that there was no denying that this was what we were called to go do.

The next few months were some of the hardest times of my life, fighting off all the negative feedback I got about taking my family to Haiti. People raised many objections: we would get sick, or it wasn't safe to bring my kids to a third world country. That trip ended up being one of the most rewarding and growing times of my life. If I had followed what others felt I should do, I would have missed this opportunity of a lifetime.

Father, help us hear you clearly. Give us dreams and visions of the call that you have for our lives. I pray that you would burn out the fear of man that plagues our lives and hold us back from reaching our full potential. God, we thank you that you never leave us nor forsake us, and I pray that you would continue to raise us up to be warriors for your kingdom. I ask you to search my heart. I ask you to fill me with your Holy Spirit and reveal to me the direction that you have for my future. I praise you. Amen.

35

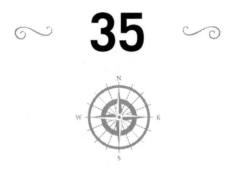

FREEDOM FROM FEAR

As a kid, I consistently struggled with fear. As I lay in bed at night, my mind would run wild with all sorts of fears, but my greatest was the fear of death. I would get to the point where I would almost have a panic attack every time my mind went there. Throughout the years, I found ways to cope with this debilitating fear. I would sing, change my thoughts to happier thoughts, or just get up and watch a movie. I got pretty good at burying all of my fears inside me.

I had no idea that there was such a thing as freedom from fear. I felt this was something I would have to carry for the rest of my life. This went on until well into my twenties and even a bit into my thirties. When I started running after God, I read the book called *Living a Life of Fire* by Reinhard Bonnke. I read about people in Africa giving their lives to Jesus and being set free from all sorts of diseases, including anxiety and depression. This book stirred up a fire in me to experience God in a more passionate way, so I applied and was given the incredible opportunity to attend the school of ministry where Reinhard Bonnke taught. Other ministers were there, including Todd White and Daniel Kolenda. They all shared radical testimonies of their ministries.

I realized that I knew a lot of facts about God, but I hadn't experienced Jesus as they had. It caused a hunger to grow inside of me. I wanted to pray for people who were sick or blind and watch Jesus heal them before my eyes.

On the final night of the school, they were going to pray over every student. The night before this, I had the biggest fear-induced panic attack I'd ever had. The Bible says in 2 Timothy 1:7 that "the Spirit God gave us does not make us timid, but gives us power, love and self-discipline." This means that such fear is a spirit, and it is not from God because God gives us a sound mind, not a fearful mind. I realized that this panic attack was Satan's attempt to take me out because he did not want me to be set free and to live a life of victory. That following night when I was prayed over, an electricity went through me that I had never experienced before. I knew from that day forward that something had changed inside me. I no longer struggle with the fear of death. Instead I now have a peace that has come over my life.

The Bible says in 2 Corinthians 3:17 that "the Lord is the Spirit, and where the Spirit of the Lord is, there is freedom." Jesus spoke to me that he cares about the whole person—not just that we are saved but that we have freedom in every area of our lives: our thought life, our health, our families, and our finances. In John 10:10 Jesus says, "The thief comes only to steal and kill and destroy; I have come that they may have life, and have it to the full." I knew that the devil was the one trying to destroy me, so once and for all, I told him to get out of my life. Jesus came for me to have fullness of life.

Jesus, I give you my life, and I ask you for this freedom to come over me. From this day forward, fear has lost its grip on me. Jesus, I pray for peace in my thought life, and I ask you to silence those fears that have been tormenting me. I ask you to come like fire and burn out anything in me that is holding me back from feeling fully alive. I ask for full freedom in every area of my life, and forgive me for believing the lies of the enemy. Jesus, thank you for restoring my life. Amen.

36

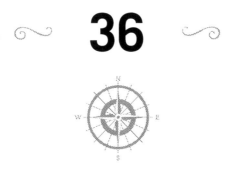

SPEAK LIFE

Proverbs 18:21 says that "the tongue has the power of life and death." This makes me think of a story that my husband's mom tells. She's shared with us about a time when she and her husband were going through a challenging season in their marriage. He was choosing the bar scene and going down a path that led him in a direction far from her and their kids. She came to feel that she had no love for him left in her. She flat-out didn't even like him anymore.

One day she cried out to God for help and decided to just speak out every day that she loved him. She didn't feel any toward him at first, but she just kept speaking it out in faith that she loved him. One day, about three weeks later when she was telling her husband that she loved him, she was shocked because her feelings for him had come back. She actually loved her husband again. I believe that her choice to speak love over her husband even when she didn't feel it saved their marriage.

In our home, we also talk about the part of our tongue that

causes death. We don't let our kids say that they are stupid, clumsy, or any other negative confession about themselves. It's amazing when you really think about how many times each day we say negative things about ourselves or our world. I catch my kids all the time saying that they hate school or that they are not good at sports. I usually catch them in their words and make them switch it to a positive comment. There is a lot of truth in the movie entitled *The Help*, when the one maid makes the child repeat after her every morning that she is kind, she is smart, and that she is important. The Bible says in Job 22:28 (KJV) that you shall decree a thing, and it shall be established. My husband was told every day by his mom that he could do all things through Christ who gave him strength. To this day, he really believes that he can do anything. There isn't a job that he can't do or a business he can't run.

I want to spend my life declaring life over myself and my family. The most powerful way to speak life over our situations is by speaking the Word of God. I speak out what the Bible says about my life. It says that "my God will meet all [my] needs according to the riches of his glory in Christ Jesus" (Philippians 4:19). It says that I am redeemed from the curse because Jesus bore my sickness and carried my diseases in his own body; by his stripes, I am healed (Isaiah 53:4–5). Philippians 1:6 says that "he who began a good work in [me] will carry it on to completion until the day of Christ Jesus." "all your children will be taught by the Lord, and great will be their peace."

Jesus, forgive me for the words that I have spoken over myself and my family that don't bring life. I choose to speak life-giving words. I ask you to remind me when harsh words come out. I pray blessings over myself and my family. I thank you for holding me and restoring my mind from every lie that I've ever believed about myself. I silence the enemy's voice over my life, and I ask you to speak truth to me. Amen.

37

SHINING BRIGHT

The other day, I was talking to one of my hair clients who had just gotten back from a trip to the Middle East. My client is not a Christian, but he began telling me about how serious the people over there are about their faith. He said it started on the flight over when there was a countdown to prayer on the movie screen ahead of them. When that countdown reached zero, he said, every head bowed down and they started to pray. Upon arrival at the airport, he noticed the prayer rooms where the people were lying face down on the ground praying.

Everywhere he went, there were people displaying their faith. Whether they were Muslim or Christian, these people were not on the fence about their faith; they were serious. He said that it wasn't like Christianity in America where many people were often casual or dismissive about their faith. He called them "on-the-couch Christians."

While listening to him talk, I was deeply convicted. I don't want to be a person who isn't oozing Jesus's love. I want people to see God's love all over me at all times. Luke 8:16 says, "No one lights a lamp and hides it in a clay jar or puts it under a bed. Instead, they put it on a stand, so that those who come in can see the light." I want to be bold enough to share my "light" with others and be sure to give him all the glory for the countless times he has rescued me, blessed us, and revealed himself to us.

I never want there to be a moment that people don't know where I stand with God. I watch many walking a walk where there is no difference between how they live and the rest of the world. They act one way around some people and another way when they are at church. This was a hard message for me to hear, but I'm realizing that in these days I need to be all in.

I needed Jesus close to me this week when I got my first mammogram and they found a spot. I also needed Jesus this week when my husband sank his brand-new excavator and also got his truck slammed into by another car. This all happened in one week, but through it all I held on to Jesus and turned my eyes to him, and he rescued us. My "spot" was not cancer, and my husband's life was spared in both accidents. I can't imagine trying to do this life on my own.

My client made an impact on me that day. It gave me a moment to evaluate where I really stood. People are watching us. Are we all in? Are we on the fence or lukewarm? God's inviting us into a relationship with him where he reveals himself to us over and over. He has revealed himself to me in such a strong way that I am all in. So let's shine bright. Let's tell the world how good he is.

Father, I thank you for rescuing me time and time again. I ask you for passion and boldness. I want to shine brightly and share your love with others. I want people to see you in my eyes, and for others to never question whether or not I follow you. I pray that you would continue to stir up that passion for you. Amen.

38

MARRIAGE

My husband and I are in our twentieth year of marriage, and this got me thinking about all the ways we have grown in the past years. We are not perfect, but we have grown into more mature people who can deal with issues in a way that is less harmful than when we first started out as newlyweds.

We got married very young, I had just turned twenty, and Charles was twenty-four. We barely had any life experience under our belts. We were in love, but both of us brought our share of baggage into the relationship. When I grew up, I had a way of never dealing with conflict. I would get upset with people, and instead of working it out, I would just ignore them until eventually those feelings of anger disappeared and we were good again. Saying sorry for me was admitting I was wrong, so I never wanted to apologize. I also had a problem with saying cutting words during arguments. I would find the words that I knew would hurt the most, not caring about the consequences of my actions, so you can imagine how our first year of marriage went.

My husband put a stop right away to my issues with conflict. He let me know that we were going to deal with our issues instead of ignoring them. I soon learned that as a rule it's better to bite my tongue than to say hurtful and cutting words. I have also gotten over my pride about always being right, so many times I am the first to say sorry. I am even willing to say sorry for things when I know I am right, just to keep the peace. I think we often feel that marriage is about feelings all the time, but many days it's our choice to stay committed that gets us through. It's hard to deny ourselves and become selfless.

Instead of waking up every morning thinking about our happiness, we can wake up thinking of ways we can bless our spouse. I love the movie *Fireproof*, where the husband decides in a last effort to save his marriage that he is going to wake up every morning for forty days to bless her. He buys her gifts, cleans for her, cooks for her, and writes her notes. He gets nothing but rejection from her, but he keeps blessing her anyway. In his selflessness, his feelings for her return, and slowly his actions start softening her heart toward him. This movie spoke to me because I had always felt that it was my husband's job to make me happy, but in reality, I am in charge of my happiness. If I am not taking care of me, then no one around me is happy.

Yesterday when my husband and I had a disagreement, I did walk away because nothing good was coming from our conversation. I know that Satan was wanting me to give up. I chose to wake up the next morning and spend time with Jesus. I read my Bible, worshipped, and prayed for my husband. Before long, all those issues I had with him from the previous night faded and love returned.

When we pursue Jesus and lay our burdens at his feet, he can replace those burdens with joy. Life can be messy, but if we stay focused on Jesus, he can turn any situation around and restore love where there is no love. He can fight our battles as we spend time worshiping. He can renew our minds and take away any thought of negativity toward our spouse that is causing destruction.

Father, I ask you to restore hope to me. I silence the enemy from causing division in my life and trying to get me to quit. I ask you to intervene on my behalf and fight my battles for me. I pray that you would restore peace in all of my relationships, and I ask you to bless my family unto a thousand generations! I thank you for the amazing people you have put into my life, and I ask you for your perfect will to be done in each one of their lives. Amen.

39

SELF-WORTH

I had a discussion earlier today with a friend about my business. I have owned a small hair shop for about twenty years now, and in that time I have never raised my prices. My friend was explaining to me how often she hears talk around the town about how inexpensive my prices are and how I should charge more.

I started to think about why I charged less, and all I could come up with was a bunch of excuses. I felt as though my shop wasn't as nice as everyone else's or that I wasn't as talented as they were. I didn't feel that I was truly professional because often I am juggling my kids' schedules, which usually makes me late in returning phone calls. I felt that if I charged less, then I wouldn't have to be as professional. When I really dissected my reasoning, it came down to the fact that I had low self-worth. I didn't feel that I was valuable enough to charge what I should.

This got me thinking about the effects of having low self-worth. If we don't have any self-worth, we will choose boyfriends/

girlfriends or spouses who are far below our standards. If we don't know that we are valuable, then we won't try for the college or career that we dream about, instead settling for a job that is below our standards. We put drugs into our body because to us, it is worth nothing. The same is true for girls going into the sex/porn industry. They have no value for themselves, so they believe it doesn't matter how they treat their bodies.

Girls and guys need to be told how valuable they are. The Bible says in 1 Peter 2:9 that "you are a chosen people, a royal priesthood, a holy nation, God's special possession, that you may declare the praises of him who called you out of darkness into his wonderful light." This means that when we invite Jesus to be Lord of our life, we are royalty. When we start seeing ourselves as valuable, then we will start acting differently.

The problem is that there are people who have grown up believing lies about themselves. They were told by parents or others in their lives that they were stupid, ugly, or lazy and that they would never amount to anything. They also believe lies that they will never meet anyone of value to marry, so they settle for the first person to come along, even if they aren't good for them. Let's start building people up. Let's tell others how valuable they are. Let's tell our children that they can be anything that they set their minds to. Let's tell them how beautiful they are and that they don't ever need to settle. Let's build them up so they don't need to look for affirmation in the wrong places.

As for me, I will raise my prices because I am worth it.

Father, show us our true value. I pray that you would replace any lie in our head with the truth. I ask you, Holy Spirit, to pour out your presence on me. I ask that you would speak truth to my children and that they would never settle for anyone or anything in their lives. I pray that you would show me ways to be an encourager to those around me. Help me be a lifter of heads, and I ask you for forgiveness for the times I have torn others down. Jesus, today I recommit my life to you, and I thank you for cleansing me. Amen.

40

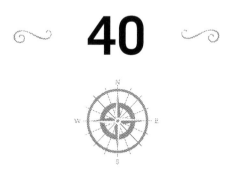

DECLUTTER

I just recently watched a show on Netflix about organization. It's about a foreign lady who goes into people's homes and helps them declutter and clean their belongings. She tells the homeowners to put all of their belongings into a pile and then get rid of the items that don't make them happy. They put back the items that they are keeping in a more organized way. At the end of the show, the homeowners are much more relaxed in their house and at peace because they aren't being overtaken by their stuff anymore. They aren't wasting so much time looking for their things because their belongings are clearly visible and not cluttered by unnecessary junk.

This show has completely inspired me. I have spent the past couple of days going through my belongings and decluttering. My kitchen is so much more user friendly now that you can look into the drawers, cabinets, and pantry and see what is inside them without digging around for utensils. It used to take me forever to find the measuring spoons and bowls when I tried to bake. The same would happen as I got dressed in the morning; I was spending lots of unnecessary time looking for the shirt or pants that I was hoping to wear that day. But now that I have organized, there is definitely a greater sense of peace in my home. I won't dread cookie baking anymore because there won't be any time wasted digging around for my things.

On my walk today I was thinking about how this applies to all areas of our lives. The Bible says in John 15:2 that the Father "cuts off every branch in [Jesus] that bears no fruit, while every branch that does bear fruit he prunes so that it will be even more fruitful." It's really good to look over our lives to see which areas need to be "pruned." Is your day getting cluttered by TV and social media? Do you own so much stuff that you are wasting time maintaining the things that you own? Are you wasting money and resources on things that aren't necessary? Someone once told me that every time you buy something, you should take into consideration the amount of time and money it will take to maintain it and consider if you have that time to spare. In our business, we have had to prune employees by removing the ones who weren't being fruitful to make room for the ones that were going to flourish working for us. I struggle with the pruning process. During my time of organizing, I struggle because I don't like the mess of my house during the process because it gets even messier. That stage of pulling out my stuff and having a bit of chaos is necessary to get to my intended result of organization. If we are remodeling our house, it gets pretty messy before the project is actually completed. The same is true for organizing my time. It's painful for me to cut down on things like late-night TV watching, but the result is that I am able to wake up early and pray for my family, which is very important for me to do in this season of my life.

As the lady instructed us to do in my show, I am going to

organize every area of my life. I am going to get rid of the things that aren't necessary. The most important time in my day is my time praying and reading the Bible in the morning. Next, I want to make sure I am spending enough quality time connecting with my family. I am looking at all the areas that I am focusing on this year, whether in our business or home, and I am going to remove the unnecessary time wasters.

Father, help me prioritize my life, my time, my stuff, and the things that are important to me. Show me the areas of my life that are stealing my energy and my time. Show me the areas that are even "good" things but should not be my priority in this season. Thank you for helping me declutter during this time and bringing a greater level of peace into my home and into every area of my life. Amen.

41

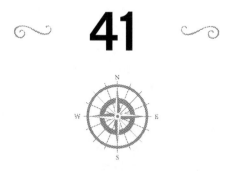

EMPTINESS

Do you feel empty inside? Do you feel as if you're living a life that is lifeless and has no meaning? You go to a job every day just to make money, come home to make dinner, and go to bed, only to do the same things the next day. You have lost the joy and have no ounce of hope left for anything great to happen in your life. You have jumped into the vicious cycle of routine, and you are exhausted.

I was at that place in life about ten years ago when I cried out to God for help. I wrote in my journal that I needed God to pull me up out of my pit of depression. Jesus heard my cry for help, and he rescued me. You see, Jesus is the *only* thing that will fill that emptiness inside. We try to fill that emptiness with countless other things like alcohol, movies, relationships, or even drugs. Jesus is the only way to have out-of-this-world peace in your mind, joy in your heart, and freedom from depression. He is the *way*, the *truth*, and the *life* (John 14:6).

I grew up in the church. I knew how to give my life to Jesus and knew that I needed to ask him to come into my life if I wanted to go to heaven. I knew that I needed to cry out to God and ask him to cleanse me from all my sins and invite him into my life. However, I realized that there are people who have never heard about Jesus and have no idea the hope that is available if they seek him out and pursue a relationship with him.

I started my relationship with him by desperate cries in my journal. I started running after him. I was passionate about going to church every Sunday, and I also started waking up every morning and going on "prayer walks." I would simply take a walk and talk to God, and I would tell him about things. He radically filled my life with hope and purpose.

Now I have a fire and passion in me, but I also have a problem with forgetting that there may be people who need to fill that void also. Start by giving God a chance. Ask him into your life. Pursue a relationship with him. Ask him to fill you with joy and peace, and tell the anxiety, worry, and fear to get out of your life for good.

Father, I ask you to come into my life. I want to pursue a deeper relationship with you. I ask you to forgive me of my sin and heal my heart from every painful experience that I've had. Come and fill me with hope again. Thank you for that peace that only comes from you. I ask you to make yourself real to each and every one of us and to fill that emptiness inside with your Holy Spirit. Amen.

42

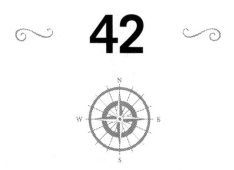

BOYS AND SHOPPING

This morning I was thinking about my girls and their shopping habits. My middle daughter is the pickiest of all of them. She will spend an entire day deciding on the perfect shoes to buy. She takes weeks to shop for school clothes and even longer to pick out the perfect prom dress. She is very particular about everything in her life. It takes a lot of thought for her to pick out the right outfit to go with the perfect shoes, and then she even spends time picking the perfect socks. Every decision in her life is really thought out and analyzed. She even thinks out the perfect meals that she would like to have for dinner.

My oldest and youngest daughter go shopping a little differently. They both tend to see things that they *love* right off the bat and buy them instantly, especially my youngest. When we go on vacations, she will spend all her money in the first store that we go into and have no more to spend during the rest of the trip. Many times she regrets her decisions because those purchases were spontaneous.

The items grabbed her attention at first, but she took no thought about whether she really needed each item and whether she might prefer something else down the road. Unlike my middle child, she is a fly-by-the-seat-of-her-pants girl and makes quick decisions, like what to wear or how to wear her hair.

I love all of their personalities, and I'm not saying anyone is better than the others, but this analogy made me think about how we choose our spouses. I think many times in choosing a husband or a wife, we take the approach of my younger daughter's shopping habits. We see someone who looks appealing right off, "try them on," and then suffer the consequences of our decisions later on. We see someone who looks appealing on the outside, but then we don't take into consideration how that person may be long term.

Maybe we need to take my middle daughter's approach in choosing a significant other. All too often we are spontaneous shoppers, and if we took the time to think about our decisions before we jumped in, we could save some heartache along the way. We need to put some thought into it. *How does this person treat me? Are they emotionally unstable? Does this person actually have good character or just a pretty face? Can I see them as a good parent, or will they grow into a deadbeat?* I even see many people choosing boyfriends or girlfriends or spouses because they don't want to be alone. They think it's better to have even a dud person than no person at all, so they settle.

So here is my advice. Pick someone with good character, not just a pretty face. Pick someone who spoils you, who leaves you no doubt that he or she has eyes only for you. Don't pick someone if you have to question their loyalty. Pick someone who has the same values as yours. Pick someone you can see as an amazing parent someday. Pick someone who is kind and emotionally stable. But above all else, pray for the perfect person to complement your life.

Father, you know the perfect companion to complement my life. I pray that you would protect me from those influences that are trying to kill, steal, and destroy my life. I pray for your wisdom and discernment in choosing a spouse. I pray that all my decisions will honor you. I love you, Jesus, and I want to give you every part of my life. Amen.

43

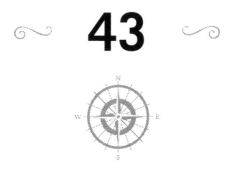

CAST YOUR CARES

A few days ago, I woke up in the middle of the night in a panic. I had a lot on my mind, and I started trying to figure everything out on my own. More anxious thoughts crowded in, and then I started to worry that things in our life were just going to fall apart. I was worrying about whether our daughter was choosing the right college and questioning the decisions we were making in our business. Those thoughts led to other thoughts, and pretty soon I was wrapped up in fear.

I got out of bed at that point and headed to the spot in the living room where I journal and read my Bible. The Bible says to cast all your cares onto the Lord, so I got out my journal and listed all the things that I was overanalyzing. I listed out all the worries over my daughter going off to college and all our financial decisions, as well as each child and the concerns I had for them. Anything I had on my mind, I put it on the paper and then prayed that God would take these concerns from me. I prayed that he would take these precious people in my life and make all things work together for good. I prayed that God would carry the burdens that I was trying to carry on my own.

I was trying to fix everything in my own strength, but people were never meant to do that. The Bible says in Philippians 4:6 to "be anxious for nothing, but in everything by prayer and supplication, with thanksgiving, let your requests be made known to God" (NKJV). Then, sure enough, after I gave all my worries to God, I felt peace, and the worries left. I was able then to fall asleep and get a good night's rest. If I hadn't done that, I would have spent the entire night trying to analyze and fix everything in our life.

I refuse to let worry run my life, so when those thoughts of worry come in, I will continue to give them over to God. The battlefield is in our thought life, and we need to take control of those negative and anxious thoughts. Philippians 4:8 says, "Whatever is true, whatever is noble, whatever is right, whatever is pure, whatever is lovely, whatever is admirable—if anything is excellent or praiseworthy— think about such things." The promise in the next verse is that "the God of peace will be with you."

Jesus, we need you to come and transform our thought life. Wash our minds clean from any tormenting thoughts, and I ask you to fill our minds with peace. I cast all my cares onto you, Jesus, and I pray that you would make all things work together for good in my life and in my family's lives. I pray that you would carry my burdens and heal any sickness. Jesus, I thank you for taking care of our needs and giving us peaceful sleep. Father, I place _____ in your hands, and I pray that you would do an amazing miracle in their life. I give you _____ (this need) and I pray that your hand would be on this situation. Thank you for being so faithful, and I praise you for being such a good Father. Amen.

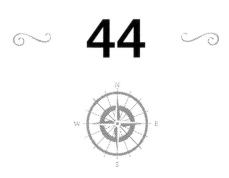

44

INFLUENCE

I was talking to my sister recently about how she just started running consistently every day. She told me how hard it was at first, but after a while it became less and less of a dread. I left that conversation feeling inspired. I left wanting to become a runner as well.

This conversation got me thinking a lot about influence. In this life, we are influencing others all the time. Are we influencing others for good or bad?

There are people all around who are influencing others in a negative way. They try to pull others into their negative lifestyles by drawing them into their sin. We see kids all the time trying drugs for the first time under the influence of another. We see people encouraging others into gossip or pornography every day. Many times, people like to bring others down to their level to make them feel less guilty about where they are in their life. The Bible says in

Proverbs 13:20 (KJV), "He that walketh with wise men shall be wise: but a companion of fools shall be destroyed."

I want to live a life that points people to Jesus. I want to live a life that is always encouraging and uplifting. The legacy that I want to leave is one that influences others for good. I want the life that I live to encourage others to live their best life. Ephesians 5:1–4 says,

> Follow God's example, therefore, as dearly loved children and walk in the way of love, just as Christ loved us and gave himself up for us as a fragrant offering and sacrifice to God.
>
> But among you there must not be even a hint of sexual immorality, or of any kind of impurity, or of greed, because these are improper for God's holy people. Nor should there be obscenity, foolish talk or coarse joking, which are out of place, but rather thanksgiving.

When people walk away from you, are they left encouraged, or do you leak negativity on to them? I love that this passage says to let worship fill your heart and to spill out in your words.

Father, I pray that the words of my mouth are acceptable to you. I pray that my life would be an encouragement to those around me and that I would imitate you, God, in everything that I do. Father, forgive me for the times when I may have wrongly influenced those that are around me. I pray that you would steer those people that I have wronged to the right path. Jesus, I need you to fill me up with your love so that I can spill it out to those I come into contact with. I want to encourage people in their parenting, their marriage, their walk with Jesus, and in their everyday life. May I never steer another in any other direction other than yours, Jesus. I pray that the life I live would be an example that is worth following. Amen.

45

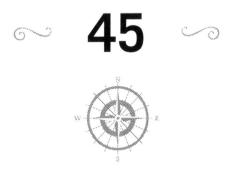

USE YOUR AUTHORITY

As a kid, I had to walk to and from school every day. The bad part of walking to school was that on most days, I would get chased by stray dogs in the neighborhood. I quickly learned that if I yelled at the dogs in a stern, authoritative tone to go home, they would listen and turn the other way. If I talked to the dog in a quiet, scared tone, the dog would continue to harass me.

Fast-forward twenty-plus years to now, and we have our own dog that we are training. Our dog listens only to my husband, who uses an authoritative tone with him, as I tend to be the nice one who only talks to him in a sweet tone and lets him get away with everything. The dog knows that he can't get away with being naughty around my husband. Through having these dogs in my life, God is teaching me that we need to use our authority to trample the devil under our feet (Romans 16:20).

Much like the stray dogs from my childhood, the devil is always there trying to get a foothold in your life. He will use any avenue he can to try and kill, steal, and destroy your life. He will try and get at your finances, your mind, your loved ones, or your physical health to try to destroy your life. The good news is that the Bible says that Jesus came to give us life abundantly (John 10:10).

Jesus said that this authority has been given to us, so it's our job to take authority over those things that are coming against our abundant life. It's our job to open up the doors to our homes and tell the devil to get out! Tell him with authority to get his hands off your kids, your health, and your finances. Instead of getting overcome by worry, put those worries in Jesus's hands and speak out. Declare "In Jesus's name, get out of my life!" Ephesians 6:12 says that "our struggle is not against flesh and blood, but against the rulers, against the authorities, against the powers of this dark world and against the spiritual forces of evil in the heavenly realms."

So instead of acting the sweet innocent as I do with my dog, letting him get away with everything, take authority over the devil, and put him under your feet once and for all.

Jesus, I thank you that you are Lord over my life and that you care about every area of my life. I thank you for abundant life, and I cast all my cares onto you. I pray that you would put a shield of protection around my life and my family's lives. I pray that you would bring restoration to every area where the devil has come and tried to steal from us. I thank you that your Word says that no weapons that are formed against us will prosper. Amen.

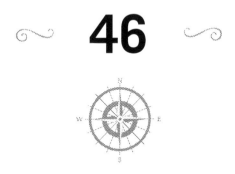

46

EARNESTLY SEEKING

The verse Hebrews 11:6 has been coming to mind a lot lately. It says that "without faith it is impossible to please God, because anyone who comes to him must believe that he exists and that he rewards those who earnestly seek him." In our lives, it is crucially important that we earnestly seek God. In a culture that earnestly seeks money, pleasure, fame, attention, comfort, and popularity, it's easy for us to get drawn into focusing on those as well. But Hebrews states that God rewards those who earnestly seek him. Are we taking time to be still and focus on God? Are we going against what our flesh wants and rising early to spend time in pursuit of God? Are we making church a priority?

There is a constant battle with ourselves to be comfortable. It's easier to stay in bed and watch movies instead of waking early on a Sunday to pursue God. It's comfortable to our flesh to watch our late-night TV instead of watching a sermon before bed, but I would rather be found earnestly seeking God. I want to read my

Bible and pray when only God is watching. I want to be faithful to seek him even when I don't have a massive God encounter. I want to be diligent to pray even when I don't see the answers manifesting yet. I want to take the time to help people even when nobody else is watching. We need to live to please God and not man.

Father God, thank you for your Word, which comes alive every time I read it. Forgive me for not always seeking you in my life. I pray that you would gently remind me always to seek you first. Give me the passion to make seeking you the priority. Give me the fire that sustains me even during the hard times and the endurance to resist my desire to choose the comfortable route. I want to be found seeking you with my whole heart, and I pray that you would make yourself more and more known to me. Amen.

47

USE YOUR WORDS WISELY

God's been speaking to me recently about my words and about guarding myself from gossip and slander. It's easy to have opinions about others and to gossip about them and judge them. The ninth commandment in the Bible says not to bear false witness. This means speaking falsely in any matter—lying, equivocating, and any way devising and designing to deceive our neighbor. It also means speaking unjustly against our neighbor.

In my business as a hairdresser, I am using my words all day long. I can use my words to encourage others and build them up, or I can use them to tear others down. I am always listening to that voice inside me that says, "Maybe you shouldn't talk about others like that," the voice that says, "Shhh, change the subject." I think we often enjoy talking negatively about others because somehow it makes us feel better about ourselves. But I would rather have God trust me to use my words to build others up and to encourage them.

When I was a kid, I got caught repeating gossip about a girl in my English class. The teacher told my mom how I was talking badly about this other girl. My mom approached me about my words and was pretty ashamed of how I had acted. I was disappointed with myself, and that moment marked me because I realized how bad it feels to get caught in your negative words. I see kids every day getting caught talking badly about their friends behind their backs or reading texts about negative things they have said about their friends.

So here are some words of wisdom from this mama. If you wouldn't say it to their face, don't say it. Do to others what you would want done to you. Friends don't talk badly about their friends behind their backs. Choose friends who build you up rather than tear you down. When you feel that gentle nudge to change the course of your conversation, change it. Don't text negative words about your friends. Let's be people who are loyal and full of integrity.

Father, forgive me for my negative words. I pray that you would cleanse me from all unrighteousness. I pray that you would continue to guide me and help me use my words to build people up rather than tear others down. Give me the strength to change the course of my conversation when gossip arises, and help me grow to be a person who uses my words only to encourage others. Amen.

48

MUSCLE MEMORY

When I was in high school, I played basketball. The position I played was shooting guard, which meant I had to make sure that I had a pretty good shot. I would spend hours and hours in the gym shooting. Even in the offseason, I would spend so much time practicing that my shot was almost perfect just using muscle memory. I didn't have to think about my form anymore because I had spent so much time doing it the right way that my body just knew how to do it right. I could shoot three-pointer after three-pointer, and they would go in.

I wonder how we could use muscle memory with the rest of our lives. How would our lives change if we took the time to train ourselves until we had muscle memory? What if we formed good habits for ourselves by training our bodies to do new things?

When we are learning new things, we always go through a tough period at the start. For instance, when I wanted to start waking up early to spend time reading my Bible and praying, I really struggled with wanting to sleep in. But now over time, my body is trained to wake up, and I really look forward to my Jesus and coffee time in the mornings. When I learned to play the piano, I got frustrated in the beginning because my fingers weren't trained yet to hit those notes. When I was learning to cut hair, I got frustrated because I had to hold the scissors the exact opposite way that I had grown accustomed to. But now that I have been doing hair for twenty years, I don't even think about it, and when I sit to play the piano, I don't think about it and simply play.

The Bible has a story about two guys named Caleb and Joshua. Caleb and Joshua were selected with ten other men to go and explore the Promised Land after Moses had led the Israelites out of Egypt, through the Red Sea and into the wilderness. The report that came back about the Promised Land was that it was amazing, flowing with milk and honey, but the people who lived there seemed scary and large. This report frightened everyone except Caleb and Joshua. They urged the people not to be afraid to follow what God had for them, and said that if God called them to do something, then they should follow. The end of the story states that Caleb and Joshua were the only two who weren't led by fear. The Bible even says, "Because my servant Caleb has a different spirit and follows me wholeheartedly, I will bring him into the land he went to, and his descendants will inherit it" (Numbers 14:24; see also verse 30). Caleb and Joshua were faithful and trusted God. Fear didn't hold them back.

What if we practiced being faithful and didn't let fear stop us from stepping out and trying something new? What if we practiced the right habits so much that we just had "muscle memory"? What kind of person do you want to be, and what new habits would you like to implement into your life? I want to be caught being faithful and fearless like Caleb and Joshua. I want to be so bold, kind, giving, and helpful that it just becomes who I am without even thinking about it. I want to step out and pray for others so much that the fear of ministering to others just dissolves.

Father, I ask you for more boldness and tenacity in my life. I pray that I would never be the type of person who just quits when things get hard or is afraid to try something new. I pray for strength to make it through the hard times. Thank you for always being with me; you are so faithful. Amen.

49

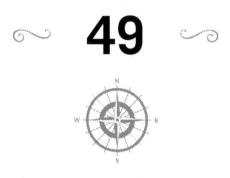

TEENAGERS

When we become Christians, we enter into a relationship with God. The more time we spend pursuing our relationship with God, the less we will focus on ourselves and the more we'll focus on those around us. When we first give our lives to follow Christ, we are not expected to know anything except that Jesus is the Way, the Truth, and the Life. At that point, we are spiritual babies who need to be fed spiritual milk, and like real babies, we need to be helped and cared for. First Peter 2:2–3 exhorts us, "Like newborn babies, crave pure spiritual milk, so that by it you may grow up in your salvation, now that you have tasted that the Lord is good."

Teenagers by nature tend to be pretty self-focused. As a teenager, I was concerned with my spot on my basketball team, boys, and my clothes. I rarely thought about the other lives that I wanted to impact or world problems. Whenever I made money, I always thought about what kind of clothes I was going to buy for myself, and I never thought about ways that my money could be used to help others. I was easily offended when people said bad things about me, and I was quick to gossip about those who had offended me. For most teenagers, selflessness doesn't exist.

Unfortunately, many of us Christ-followers get stuck in the "teenager" part of our walk with God. We are so inwardly focused that we forget to look outward. We get offended by our pastor or other members of the church, and then we are quick to leave and find another church when things don't go our way. We may talk badly about our pastors when they go an extra ten minutes over their sermon time. We quit the minute things get hard in life instead of persevering during the hard times. I notice that often, when people are stuck in the teenage stage, they only want to talk about themselves and their problems instead of how to influence others for good.

When I grew up and had children of my own, I shed any ounce of selfishness that I had. I was fully focused on my babies and their well-being. Sleep became nonexistent, and I was okay with that because I was being a mother, and my babies were more important than myself. It was more fun to buy things for my kids than to buy clothes for myself, and tuition to preschool and dance lessons became more important than my beloved trips to Mexico.

Just as I had to grow up as a mom, God is calling us as a body of Christ to grow up. If we shift our eyes off of ourselves and onto Him, we will become more mature. Real change happens when we spend time with God, reading his Word, being still, worshipping him, praying to him, and fellowshipping with other believers.

I never want to stop growing. I want to become a person who is hard to offend and is quick to bless others. I want to be quick to serve at church and never critical about those around me. I want to be quick to listen if God instructs me to give money. I also want to be a good listener and fully compassionate about those around me. First Corinthians 13:11 says that "when I was a child, I thought like a child, I reasoned like a child. When I became a man, I put the ways of childhood behind me."

Jesus, help us to grow up. Help us to be fully mature and to get our eyes back on you and away from our circumstances. I ask you, Holy Spirit, to speak to us about ways in which we can grow to become more and more like Christ. Come, Holy Spirit, and have your way in my life. Amen.

50

DISCIPLINE

Lately I've been noticing a trend in the United States of running after a comfortable lifestyle. We want all the comforts of life without working hard for them. We want to be fit without working out and eating healthy. We want to have a deep relationship with Jesus without working to spend time with him. We want to have a close relationship with our kids without working on the relationship. We want the big, fancy house without working for it. We want to become a doctor without going to college. It has become so easy to spend time on our phones and watching Netflix that we forget to spend time on ourselves and our relationships.

The Bible says in 1 Corinthians 9:27 that Paul disciplined his body like an athlete, training it to do what it should. In some translations it says that he toughened his body with punches and made it his slave.

Of course, nobody wants to wake up early and exercise. Nobody wants to pick the salad over the donut. Nobody wants to set the alarm an hour early to make time to spend with Jesus. It's easier to press snooze. It's easier to watch Netflix than to spend time with the family. It's easier to quit your job than to work, and it's certainly easier to drop out of college than to study hard.

We need to get a mental picture of the type of life we want to live and go for it! Get a mental picture of the person you want to be, and go for it. If it's a fit and healthy person, then glue that image in your head, and decide to exercise every day, one day at a time. If it's a close relationship with Jesus, make a decision to spend time with him every day by reading the Bible, praying, listening to worship music in the car, or even journaling your thoughts to him. If you want an amazing career, study hard for it! If you want a spouse who takes care of themselves physically ... take care of yourself. Put down the phones, and work hard for what you want. Spend time with your kids. Get off the couch and move. If you want deeper relationships, be a friend who puts in time working on them. If you want to be a better spouse, spend more time one on one with your spouse without any distractions. Too often quality time has turned into two people going on devices at the same time while sitting next to each other.

Lord, help us manage our time. Help us not to be comfortable. Help us not to take the easy road. Train us to be disciplined like Paul. I pray that we never become lazy or complacent. Give us dreams and goals for our lives, and help us lay aside any distractions that are holding us back. Father, help us become the world changers that you have created us to be. Amen.

51

BLESS YOUR SONS
AND DAUGHTERS

I've been reading through the Old Testament lately. I tend to be a New Testament girl, but recently I've been feeling led to dig deep into the Old Testament. Something that has stood out to me while reading is the importance of speaking blessings. Even back in those days, they understood the importance of speaking blessings over their children. Joseph's father made a point of sitting his sons down before he died and speaking blessings over them.

This makes me think about the kinds of words we are speaking over our children. Joseph's father spoke over him, saying,

> "Joseph is a fruitful tree, a fruitful tree by a spring, with branches climbing over a wall. Archers provoked him, shot at him, and attacked him. But his bow stayed steady, and his arms remained

limber because of the Mighty One of Jacob, because of the name of the Shepherd, the Rock of Israel, because of the God of your father who helps you, blessings from the heavens above, blessings from the deep springs below the ground, blessings from breasts and womb. The blessings of your father are greater than the blessings of the oldest mountains and the riches of the ancient hills. May these blessings rest on the head of Joseph, on the crown of the prince among his brothers." (Genesis 49:22-24, God's World Translation).

These are beautiful words declared over a son. I would like to make sure I have my own declarations for my children that are blessings for them rather than cursing.

How often do we have to catch ourselves before speaking words like "I'm not sure if they are ever going to figure their life out" or "that kid of mine can't seem to make any good decisions at all"? Instead, I would like to say, "Everything that my children touch will be blessed. My grandchildren will be blessed and follow after God all of their days. My children will be healthy and strong, and no sickness will come upon them. My children will marry godly spouses, and they will love and serve Jesus together."

If those in the Old Testament knew the importance of blessing the next generation, then we should take note and follow. Let's ask for forgiveness for speaking words that have not been life-giving. Let's choose this day to speak life.

Jesus, I declare that no weapon formed against my family will prosper. My children will be taught of the Lord, and great will be their peace. Father, I pray that you will bless my family from generation to generation. I pray that you will direct my family's steps. Please forgive me if I've ever spoken words over my children that do not line up with the Word. I praise you for people who have spoken life over me, and I forgive those who have spoken words over me that were not life-giving. I pray that you would release me from any negative curse that may have been spoken over my life. Father, we thank you for freedom. Amen.

52

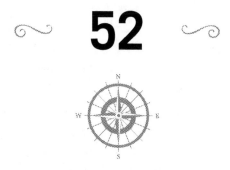

CHRISTMAS GOODNESS

Every year at Christmas, I write letters to each of my three girls and put them in their stockings. I write to let them know how proud I am of all of them in their own different ways. I want to pull out the good in them to let them know that I see it. I don't want to just point out the things they aren't doing; I want to point out things like being kind, friendly, helpful, and generous, qualities that can sometimes be overlooked.

This year, as I've been reflecting on my kids, I realize just how different and unique we all are. For kids living on a small island, it's hard sometimes because there aren't as many different options of sports and activities to try out. The main sports here are basketball, volleyball, baseball, wrestling, cheer, dance, and music. That sounds like a lot of options, and it is, but not every kid fits into one of those categories. Some are amazing at reading, debate, humor, being a good friend, or public speaking. For kids, I think it's easy to measure your worth based on how good you are at a sport. And if you aren't athletic in a sea of athletes, it could get frustrating. My three girls are different in every way. One of my oldest daughter's awesome qualities is that she is incredibly funny. While I've been healing from my hysterectomy, I have had to tell her many times to stop talking because I couldn't laugh so much. My middle daughter is helpful and kind, and she is always helping me around the house. I often think she is more responsible than I am. My youngest has the most amazing imagination I have ever seen. I feel she could run an orphanage as an eight-year-old. I love how every night she prays for the poor and homeless. They are so uniquely different and amazing in their own way. We may not always be the best athlete or the most academic, but a lot of our gifts can't be measured.

I'm hoping in my life to start pulling out the gold in everyone— not pointing out the junk all the time, but to pointing out the goodness. There was a song a while back that says, "They will know we are Christians by our love" (not judgment). I also don't want to get frustrated trying to be someone that I am not. I want to be happy with who I am and start seeing other people the way God sees them: full of goodness! What a great time like Christmas to invite Jesus to come into your life and see the amazing destiny and transformation that takes place!

Father, help us see those around us through your eyes. Forgive us if we have ever cast judgment toward them. Help us love as you love, and show us the gold in those around us. Give us boldness to encourage and build up our neighbors and family. Thank you for increasing our wisdom and love. Amen.

53

THE IMPORTANT THINGS

There's a song by Alabama that says, "I'm in a hurry to get things done, I rush and rush until life's no fun …." I'm going through a time of prioritizing my life. I notice that it's really easy to start adding more and more things to my plate; before long, I don't even recognize myself. I'm just going from one thing to the next, then by the time my family gets me at the end of the night, I'm just a vegetable on the couch with only enough energy to lift a remote control.

It's always good for me to self-reflect before I get way off course. My pastor says examining yourself is like looking at a compass; it's always good to keep checking, or before long, you are completely off course, going entirely in the wrong direction. In the same way, I think it's good to always have your main priorities in mind and constantly reflect on them to make sure you aren't completely off course to what you want in life.

In my life, my top three priorities are God, my husband, and my kids. But lately, lots of other things have been jumping ahead of those three. The Bible says to seek first God's kingdom and righteousness, and then "all these things shall be added unto you" (Matthew 6:33 KJV). I never want to get that verse switched around. I hear many people say, "When this or that happens, then I will seek God," or "When my life slows down, then I will seek God." I want to seek him first before all things. I noticed that when I started seeking him then "these things" started falling into place.

Distractions creep in subtly, and before you know it, your prayer life gets shoved to the side. It's a battle to keep those priorities in place, but I never want to go back to that place of dryness in my faith. God has rescued me from a lot and helped me come out of a place of depression where I never want to go again. That is something that wakes me up every morning. I need him to help me live my life, and the more I spend time with him, the better I know him and the direction he wants for my life.

Just as I need to spend time with Jesus for our relationship to grow, I need to spend time with my husband. It's really easy to put him last. If I never communicated with him, I think we would just go off in different directions and lead two different lives. I've been thinking about Gary Chapman's book *The Five Love Languages*. The first chapter talks about a husband and wife who are getting a divorce. He's confused about why things fell apart, because he brought her flowers all the time. But she is not a gift person, and she's been missing some quality time with her husband.

The five love languages are physical touch, quality time, words of affirmation, gifts, and acts of service. I have to remember that we all receive love differently. What may be important to me might not be important to the other person. I may go home every night and do the dishes for my husband and think that I'm being loving, but it may not mean much to him. Lately, I have to be intentional about our relationship because if I'm exhausted after a long day, then he is lucky that I pick up the phone to order a pizza!

My kids are another main priority of mine. I love all three of them very much, and I know my days with them in our house are limited. I want to influence them as much as I can in the time that I have left with them. I want to have a connection with them, take them on trips, and teach them to be good people. I want to always be in the place with them that they want to obey me because they love me, not because I'm mean and controlling. I want them to know that I'm proud of them, not because of what they do but because they are my kids and I love them.

However, that relationship building takes time, something I have to fight for every day. I may need to turn off Facebook more, say no to business and volunteer opportunities and nights out with friends, or change up my work schedule. But at the end of the day, I want to be able to say that I ran my race well. When my kids leave home, I will have no regrets, and my husband and I will be able to celebrate many, many, many anniversaries.

Matthew 6:33 says, "Seek first his kingdom and his righteousness, and all these things will be given to you as well. Father, we ask you to help us take control of our time. Help us to set our schedules with you as our top priority. Forgive us if we have gotten off course. We want to run our race well, but for us to do that, you must help us get our priorities straight. We love you, Jesus, and we need your presence in our lives. Amen.

54

STARTING FIVE

When I was in high school, I played basketball. The goal was to be on the starting five, the first five players to be on the court at the beginning of the game. I put everything into basketball, and it was the most important thing to me back then. I never thought about life ten years down the road; it was all about being in the moment and making the starting five. A couple of times I actually did it, and life was good, but there were many times where I had my share of sitting on the bench.

When I had kids of my own, I assumed they would have the same interests as I had. But the funny thing that I'm learning is how different we all are. I have three girls who are all completely different. Now that two of them are in high school, I'm having fun discovering how uniquely and wonderfully they are different. My oldest is naturally smart and outgoing, an awesome friend, and very forgiving. She only did sports for the social aspect and less for the actual sport; she's an amazing writer, and we have recently discovered that she is an amazing singer.

My second daughter is just like me; very much into sports, super kind, a hard worker, and more of a smaller crowd kind of girl. So far, my youngest is very social, super into pretend, but more into music than the other two. I'm excited to see who they end up becoming.

I have been saying to them lately that we can't all be starting five at everything. When they get frustrated about not getting on the team as they expected to, we talk about how this world would be pretty boring if we were all alike and all starting five basketball. I'm not saying that they shouldn't do what they want to do and work hard and improve and reach goals, but I do think that there is a terrible epidemic of comparison in our world. We need to have the starting five writers, singers, and mathematicians step up to be who they were created to be. It gets frustrating when we start comparing ourselves with others instead of embracing who we are.

Psalm 139:13–14 says that God "created my inmost being; you knit me together in my mother's womb." It says that we are fearfully and wonderfully made! Let's stop wishing we were someone else and use who we are to help better the kingdom! Let's grow and discover new giftings that we never knew we had! Let's encourage others who may not have discovered who they are yet!

Father, we thank you that you made us so different and unique. I pray that you would open our eyes to the gifts and talents that you have blessed us with. Show us the beautiful qualities that make us unique. Your handiwork is unfathomable. We praise you for adding so much beauty to this world. Amen.

55

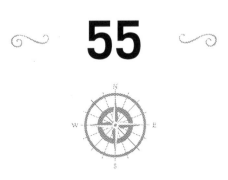

MERMAIDS

My youngest daughter woke up this morning super excited because at swim class today she and her friends were going to be able to play mermaids. This was a big deal for me because usually it's like pulling teeth to get her out of bed. I have to go back into her room several times to make sure she is at least moving around and trying to wake up while she is groaning about how much she doesn't want to go to school, so I was pleasantly surprised at how quickly she got up today.

Then I felt the Lord speak to me about having a vision for our life. He spoke to me about how when we have hope and excitement for the day, it's easy to get out of bed. The opposite is true too, though; when we have no vision or hope for our life, it makes getting out of bed in the morning torture.

The Bible says that without vision, God's people perish. I remember having my first job at a barbershop in my twenties. This particular shop was slammed busy all the time, so I was having a hard time balancing my life. I always felt overscheduled, which made it really hard to find time to take care of myself. Exercising became nonexistent in those days, and slowly I found myself gaining more and more weight. It was easier just to grab a quick Costco muffin between appointments than make anything with any nutritional value.

I let it get to the point where I didn't like what I saw in the mirror, and I stayed that way until my second daughter was born. Then it occurred to me that I wanted my kids to be proud of who I was and that I didn't want them to be embarrassed about how I looked. I got a vision of the kind of mom I wanted to be for my kids. I kept that vision in view, and that got me focused on getting my act together and taking care of myself. I started by going for walks consistently every day; then I worked up to more of an aerobic workout. That vision of being a fit mom got me out of bed every morning, and the consistency started paying off.

I spent a long-time lacking hope and vision for my life. I fought low-grade depression for many years, but when I started pursuing God, my life started changing. I decided I needed to start getting regular with my quiet times. It wasn't until I started reading my Bible, praying, and spending time just worshipping that I began feeling alive and close to God again. The closer I got to God, the better I felt, and the depression started to fall away. Now that he has encountered my life in such a real way so many times, I couldn't even imagine living my life with him far away again. That vision of how my life used to be gets me out of bed in the morning and into his presence. I never want to go back to the way things were. I also have a picture in my head of my goals for my life, my dreams, and my kids. I will wake up each day and pray for my family.

I will constantly keep the vision in front of me. I wish I'd done that when I was in high school. I think if I'd had a vision of what kind of person I wanted to be, I would have had an easier time getting out of bed in the morning. Doing homework would be easier if we had a vision of the school we want to attend or the job we want to aim for. It would be easier to work a long shift if we knew there was a purpose in it.

My husband has big dreams. He has a vision in his head of the business he wants, and it motivates him to work long hours sometimes to achieve his goals down the road. I pray that you get your excitement of life back and begin to dream again and that God gives you vision again. Even if you feel like you have fallen into a pit, God will pull you out and give you hope again. Ephesians 5:14 says, "Wake up, sleeper, rise from the dead, and Christ will shine on you."

Father, I pray that you would give us hope again. I pray that you will fill us with many dreams for our lives. I pray that we will have abundant joy and excitement for the future. I declare that your hand is upon anyone who may be feeling hopeless or depressed. I pray that your peace would fill their room and set them free. Amen.

56

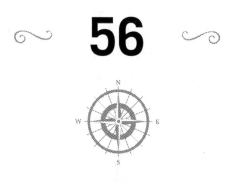

OFFENSE

Keeping people out of church due to offense is one of the biggest tactics of Satan. I often hear people tell me that they no longer attend church because the pastor said something that challenged them, or a member there said something that rubbed them the wrong way. The enemy will even put thoughts in our heads like "Nobody here likes you," or "Look at this place; it's full of hypocrites. You don't belong here." Before we know it, we have convinced ourselves that all churches are bad and that we don't need to attend.

The enemy wants to do whatever he can to keep you out of fellowship with others and out of the church, because that's how you grow. We need people to hold us accountable; to challenge us, and to worship with us. People can be tricky to be with sometimes, but we need to be around tricky people occasionally to learn to grow in our love walk. It's very easy to love happy people, but the real test of our walk with Christ is to learn to love challenging people. Luke 6:32 (NLT) says, "If you only love those who love you, why should you get credit for that? Even sinners love those who love them!" Are we learning to love? We don't have to make everyone our best friends and tell them our deepest secrets, but we can show kindness and love to everyone.

Here's my advice: fight the enemy's lies at all costs. Declare out loud, "Devil, get your hand off my life and my family's lives!" Run to a church that teaches you to have a relationship with Jesus, not just a bunch of facts about God. Find a church that teaches you that you can have your very own relationship with a God who loves you. Seek out a church that believes in the power of the Holy Spirit, because the power of God is what changes you. You don't need to spend the rest of your life battling anxiety and depression, hiding in your house because you are afraid. You need the power of God to come and set you free. You need to be around other believers who encourage you in your faith.

Fight back. Fight the urge to be lazy on Sunday mornings and sleep in. Fight the feelings of offense that are holding you back. Let them go. Be diligent. Be forgiving and strong. The Bible tells us to take no offense to a suffered wrong.

Father, help me not to get offended. Show me areas in my life where I am holding an offense. I pray that you would come in and bring healing to any hurt in my heart. Holy Spirit, come fill me. Holy Spirit, come strengthen me. I pray that I would feel alive and full of joy. I pray that nothing would hinder me from being around other believers. Father, give me boldness and confidence to be around other people who may be challenging. Help me learn to love. Amen.

57

CORONA

Right now, we are in the middle of a global pandemic. Many people are sick right now, millions are laid off work, kids are suddenly finished with school for the year, some are living in fear that they may get sick, and others are locked inside their homes facing situations that are unimaginable. Many vacations have been canceled, seniors have lost their graduations and proms, and families are forced to make decisions that they thought they would never have to make just to put food on the table. The list could go on and on about the severity of this situation. If you think about this problem long enough, it can feel overwhelming. Many are living in so much fear of their future that they feel helpless. They are watching the news all hours of the day focusing on what could go wrong. They have lost all control.

I am choosing not to focus on the storm around me. Instead of looking at the storm, I want to look to the joy that is in front of me. The Bible says in Philippians 4:6–8 not to be worried about a thing, but to be saturated in prayer throughout each day. It also says to keep your thoughts continually fixed on all that is authentic and real, honorable and admirable, beautiful and respectful, pure and holy, merciful and kind. When you are focused on the good, that doesn't mean that the bad isn't still there; it just means that you are focusing your attention on the good that is happening around you. Fear can be a sneaky thing that consumes our attention, but today I'm asking you to tell that fear to go and fix your eyes on hope.

I have lost my job for now, but instead I will be able to write more. I will be able to spend time around the campfire with my family. My family is starting to take communion every night and pray for our community and loved ones. I took a walk with my daughter yesterday and made banana bread. We have dusted off board games and art projects. We are having movie nights and bike rides.

I know there are people in much more serious situations than mine. I know that many people are stuck at home with fighting children (I remember those days). I know there are people who have lost loved ones or whose loved ones are sick. I know others who are worried about losing their businesses or homes. I am praying every night for you, and I am very sorry.

I see you. I also see an end to this. There is hope at the end. We will go back to work again, we will get our economy back, and our children will go back to school again. But in this brief pause in our lives, let's not get stressed about how much we are able to accomplish; let's take a break from the news and pick up something creative and dust it off. Let's give ourselves permission to relax. Let's reset our families and find the joy in this.

Father, we choose to cast all of our worries and anxiety onto you. I thank you for caring for us. I pray that I would always have an attitude of gratitude and thankfulness. I declare Psalm 91 over my family right now, that no sickness would come near our dwelling place. I thank you for putting your angels in charge of me and my family, to protect us in all our ways. Thank you for being my rescuer; I choose this day to put my trust in you. Amen.

58

NOTE TO SELF

There was a time while I was raising my three girls when life got a little chaotic. My girls had clashing personalities, so they fought a lot. There were days when they fought from the moment they woke up until bedtime. Mixed in with the fighting was also a bit of whining and complaining. Don't get me wrong; I loved my girls with all my heart, but there were days when I would be pulling my hair out. At my lowest point, I remember stopping in front of our daycare center in town and yelling at them, saying that if they didn't stop fighting, then they were going to get out and go in. Those were not my finest days.

My oldest daughter had such a hard time sharing that every playdate turned into a major fight. There were times when I gave up going to playgroups altogether because my children couldn't stop biting the other children. What a feeling of defeat. I remember asking myself questions like *What am I doing wrong?* or *Is this ever going to get better? Am I raising a serial killer? Will my child be able to have friends at all?* I honestly didn't know if it was ever going to get better.

I used to believe the lie that my children had to have a perfect day every day. I believed that their days needed to be filled with art projects and stimulating activities. But when my expectations weren't met and the kids ended up fighting all day, I would feel defeated. I would always declare to them, "Someday you will travel thousands of miles just to see each other!"

Fast-forward ten years, and life is very much better. The kids are actually friends, they have friends at school, there is no more biting, and the whining has decreased to a bare minimum. They actually have traveled thousands of miles just to see each other. They still have their moments, but all in all, life is much more manageable. I wish I could write a letter to my younger self and give her this advice: "This too shall pass. Your kids will get along someday. They may even become best friends. They won't wear diapers forever. Chances are, they will stop biting in grade school. The chances of them being serial killers are pretty slim. They will have friends. Life will get easier. Enjoy every moment. Have connections with your kids. Laugh, play games with them, and if you start getting frustrated, take a break. Give yourself permission to take time for yourself, and it's okay if your kids don't always have a perfect day."

Remember that our kids are the greatest gifts that we have been given.

Father, give us strength during those moments when we feel defeated. Give us patience and endurance to thrive in our parenting journey. I pray that you would guide us in making our homes full of peace and love. Thank you for the treasures that you have blessed us with, and please teach us to love well. Amen.

59

GIVING

My husband and I passed a large part of our young adult lives not very mindful of giving. Every Sunday, the offering plate was passed around, and we would throw some money in, but you couldn't say that we were tithers. The Bible calls us to take 10 percent of our earnings and give it back to God. Malachi 3:10 says to bring the whole tithe into the storehouse, that there may be food in God's house.

> "Test me in this" says the Lord Almighty, "and see if I will not throw open the floodgates of heaven and pour out so much blessing that there will not be room enough to store it."

This verse actually says to test him out. Proverbs 3:9–10 says to "honor the Lord with your wealth, with the firstfruits of all your crops; then your barns will be filled to overflowing, and your vats will brim over with new wine."

Money is mentioned over eight hundred times in the Bible, which is very informative, but the biggest change that happened for us was when my husband and I decided to be doers of the Word and not hearers only; we decided to become faithful in our giving. We wanted to try out this very important principle in the Bible. This ended up being one of the most powerful decisions we ever made. When we started radically giving, we saw God intervene in our finances in a big way. I could go on and on about all the supernatural jobs that my husband has gotten. I even had an entire thirty-thousand-dollar surgery invoice wiped out. We were handed twelve thousand dollars by a couple who wanted to pay for a mission trip to Israel for my daughter and husband to go on. I could go on for days about all the favor and blessings that have been showered on us since we started giving. I would never go back to our old ways now that I have tasted and seen that he is good.

The Bible says a lot about sowing and reaping. It states that if we plant good "seeds" then our harvest will be plentiful. What are you "planting"? Have you been reaping a good "harvest"? Are you sowing your time into good things like the Word and your family? Are you being generous instead of fearful about your money? I heard a story about a man who needed some new suits because he had become a preacher. He understood the biblical principle of sowing and reaping, so he went down and gave clothes to everyone he saw who had a need. God in return started blessing him with all sorts of suits to wear.

Do you need a turnaround in your life and in your finances? The Bible says to test God out on it. God will start intervening on your behalf in ways you've never seen. You will start seeing the turnaround that your life needs. You will see God as you haven't seen him before. Now in my life, it is a great blessing to give. I don't have the fear of sticking money in the offering plate anymore because I have seen God come through so faithfully in our lives.

Father, I thank you for the blessings and favor that you have showered upon my family and me. I thank you that you are faithful and that your kingdom principles work. Help us have the strength and passion to be generous with our money. Amen.

60

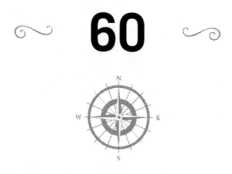

FEED YOUR FAITH

Are you feeding your faith, or are you feeding fear? We need to be feeding our faith as much as we possibly can. I love reading books about generals of the faith who watched God do many miracles through their lives. Reading about their lives stirs my faith up to get hungry and to grow deeper in my relationship with God.

Reinhard Bonnke was a missionary to Africa who watched God perform miracle after miracle as he traveled the continent preaching the gospel. Bonnke saw multitudes of people saved, healed, and delivered from demonic oppression at each of his meetings. When you hear of people's testimonies like his, your faith can't help but grow.

There are people who choose to feed their fear rather than their faith. They spend their entire days watching the news, reading articles that contradict their faith, or watching movies that are fear based. The Bible says in Philippians 4:8, "Finally, brothers and sisters, whatever is true, whatever is noble, whatever is right, whatever is pure, whatever is lovely, whatever is admirable—if anything is excellent or praiseworthy—think about such things." We are in charge of what we are filling our minds with.

We are stuck inside right now going through the coronavirus pandemic. Some people at home are constantly dwelling on all the things that could go wrong, looking up conspiracy theories, or watching the doom and gloom on the news. Those people are so worked up with fear that it's hard for them to have any faith. They are lying awake in bed every night fretting about what could go wrong. Let's switch our mind-sets; let's focus on the good. Let's build up our faith muscles.

Father, help us think about things that are lovely and turn off the negative voices that are holding us back. I pray that you will help us to build up our faith. Jesus, we love you, and we want to fill our minds with you and your goodness. Amen.

61

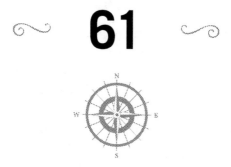

SANTA CLAUS

Many people treat their relationship with God similarly to a relationship with Santa Claus: we come to God with our lists of needs and wants every day instead of spending time seeking him and loving on him. I feel that we are being drawn into a deeper place with God in the "secret place."

I spent years not knowing how to pray. I knew that were called to pray and to seek his face, but how should I go about doing that? I had the prayer list, and I was faithful about going before God every day and telling him my needs as if he had no idea what they were. God's desire for me has been and always will be for relationship. He wants me to spend time with him, to sit in his presence, and to talk to him. When I come to him and give him my heart, pouring out my thankfulness, his presence comes and fills me with peace and joy. It's a beautiful exchange.

How about we throw away the lists for a bit and focus on his face? Turn on some soft worship music, and just sit still. Tell God how thankful you are. Offer him your heart. Give him all your cares until you have no more. Write out those little distractions that your mind keeps going to. Psalm 46:10 says to "Be still, and know that I am God." In our busy lives, it's really hard to be still. We are so used to running and running that when we finally sit still, it's really difficult. I've been waking early to seek God before all my distractions come.

How do I feel his presence? These were things people always talked about during church, but how do I experience it for myself? The Bible says we will enter his gates with thanksgiving in our hearts. When I worship him with my thankfulness and then offer up my heart, a beautiful exchange happens. I commune with the maker of the universe.

Father, teach us to pray. Teach us to have a deeper relationship with you. Teach us to feel your presence and to commune with you. We want to have a rich and full prayer life where we live under the shelter of the Most High. We don't want to be lukewarm and dry; we want to be full of life. Father, show us ways to have a more vibrant prayer life. Teach us to be still. Show us how to meet with you. Father, I thank you for making the universe yet still knowing us by name. Amen.

62

DAD

What is the image of God that is in your head? Is he angry and always ready to punish you whenever you make a mistake? Is he passive without caring about the details of your life? Is he an ultimate taskmaster, only having kids to accomplish things for him, or is he kind and loving? My pastor says often that many times we relate to God the way we relate to our natural parents. He would view God like his earthly father, who was quick to be angry every time he messed up.

The Bible says in 1 John 4:8 that God is love. The Bible explains that God has unconditional love for us. In my mind, I always felt that God would only love me if I was perfect and had my life figured out. I felt that he didn't want to be with me because my life was messy. It always seemed pretty hard to please God, but my view of God was pretty messed up. I wanted very much to please him, but I felt as if it was impossible. How many kids felt this way about their childhood families?

But in all my mess, my God still had his hand on me. He didn't take his hand off of my life because of the choices I was making. He was there and willing to clean up my messes. He put people in my life to encourage me. He was there when I was desperate and crying out to him. His love for me was not dependent on my perfection.

I'm taking a class right now from Justin and Abi Stumvoll. They cleared up some common misconceptions about God. Some lies that many people grow up believing about God are that he won't help me if I'm not doing enough right, and that he needs me to work really hard for him or the whole world will fall apart. We think God cares more about our checklist than he does about our hearts, as if he's saying, "I only love you today because I know your potential."

I want to challenge you to sit down with God and write out the lies that you have believed about his nature. Let him replace those lies with truth. He is for you. He is good. He is willing to pick you up when you fall. He will never leave you. He is there to champion you. He is pleased with you.

Father, I ask you to show me how you love me. I ask you to replace the lies I am believing about who you are. Show me people in my life who model behavior like yours. I pray that you keep making yourself real to me and connecting with me. I thank you for never leaving me and for always having your hand in my life. Amen.

63

FAITH

For my anniversary this year, my husband took me on a short boat ride to a neighboring town for dinner. Our small town is on an island with very few restaurants around, so we decided that we should go on an adventure and have dinner somewhere else. We loaded up our boat and started to head out, but as we got going, we began having some technical difficulties with our boat. Thankfully my husband can pretty much fix anything, so after tinkering with it for a few minutes, he got the boat running okay.

As we got out into the water, the wind started picking up, and we found ourselves bouncing around in our boat. My husband was super calm about the whole situation, and nothing fazed him. I was a wreck; many thoughts were crossing my mind such as the possibility that we were headed out into bad conditions, the boat might be broken, and that it could capsize from water crashing all around us. I was not calm or full of peace; I was trying to control the whole situation and convince my husband to turn around or slow down. He kept assuring me that everything was fine, that the water was not that bad, and that the best thing to do was to just keep going.

At that moment, God spoke to me. He showed me that this was what faith was. He showed me how I know nothing about boats; I don't know how to fix them or drive them. I have lived in Alaska my whole life but never even learned how to turn one on, yet when I am in a boat with my husband, I have complete faith in him that he is going to get me from point A to point B. That's how we are to have faith in God—complete trust in him. Not knowing our whole situation, we must still have faith in him.

But how was I acting? When the storm came, I was trying to control the whole situation, telling Charles what to do because of fear. I was grouchy and demanding. But really, I knew nothing about the water, how the boat should point, or what speed we should maintain, so I should just trust that he would know what was best for us.

God reminded me that we often react out of fear when the storms of life come. The opposite of fear is faith, and we need to trust God during the storms that he will see us through them, just as I had to trust Charles in that boat. The moment I had that revelation, I was able to step out of fear and enter into faith. I thanked God that he knew my situation and that I trusted him to get us where we needed to go. I just prayed that he would camp his angels around our boat at that moment. Sure enough, after a while, we got to our destination and had a great dinner.

I often think about this lesson on faith. Since that boat ride, many other "storms" have come our way—storms like financial problems, problems with our children, or concerns about our health. However, when I'm tempted to react out of fear and get super controlling or scared, I remember that, just as I had to trust Charles in the boat to get me from point A to point B, I need to trust in Jesus to see me through. "For our battle is not against flesh and blood, but against the rulers, against the authorities, against the powers of this dark world and against the spiritual forces of evil in the heavenly realms" (Ephesians 6:12).

Father, we give you our fears and ask you to turn them to faith. Forgive us for those moments when we didn't trust you. We ask you for your peace and strength to make it through the storms of life. We thank you for always guiding us and for always being there. We thank you for increasing our boldness and faith. May we always trust you with our families and our futures. We trust that you will get us to where we need to go. Amen.

64

INSIDE, OUTSIDE, UPSIDE-DOWN KINGDOM

From the outside looking in, Christianity may seem like a topsy-turvy kingdom. God says to give and then you will receive, the greatest people out there are the servants, and if you tithe, your finances will be blessed. The Bible also says to forgive your enemies and pray for those who persecute you. The Hollywood way of looking at things is to take revenge on your enemies, and you will find joy in watching them suffer. It also teaches that you shouldn't be generous because you might get burned and that if you work really hard, you will get everything you want in life.

The Bible says to seek first the kingdom of God, then all these things will be added unto you. Many times, we get that verse backward. We want all these things added unto us without seeking him first. The Bible also says to delight yourself in the Lord, and then he will give you the desires of your heart (see Psalm 37:4).

Often, we'll ask God to give us the desires of our heart without seeking him or delighting in him. If we would just learn to follow the kingdom principles in the Bible, life would work much more easily. We would save many wasted years on being bitter, sick, and financially unstable.

This inside, outside, upside-down kingdom works. Try it out! Try tithing, and watch your finances turn around. Start blessing others, and watch yourself be blessed. Try forgiving your enemies, and start living a more peaceful life in your mind. Start giving God your time, and start seeing a turnaround in your life. Start watching God give you his divine favor over your life.

Father, we trust you with our lives. We thank you for kingdom principles that work. Please remind us when we start to get things a little backward. Help us draw near to you and learn more of your divine ways. We thank you for teaching us, correcting us, and pouring out your presence on us today. Amen.

65

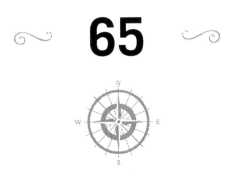

COMPARISON KILLS

The other day, I was talking to someone who was going on and on about how great this other person was. Let's call her Jane. They were praising Jane for all sorts of things, like how great her house was and how talented she was. Immediately in my mind, I started comparing myself with that Jane. *Why is my house not as clean as Jane's, why am I not working as much as Jane, or why am I not as talented as Jane?* When someone else is praised, we may feel as if something is wrong with us. In a strange way, I felt like there was a competition between me and Jane.

I also started thinking about the flip side, like when someone comes up to you and starts talking about how bad someone else is. Once someone started telling me all sorts of bad things about someone I'll call Sue. They told me how horrible Sue was as a mom; her house was always messy, and her kids seem to be having all sorts of trouble. The problem is that instead of having compassion for Sue, many people feel a little bit better about themselves because hearing about someone's faults somehow elevates us up a little. We tell ourselves, *At least I'm not like that, and I have my stuff together a little better than Sue does.* I'm realizing how dangerous this is. Comparison kills.

We are all uniquely and wonderfully made. We all have different giftings and strengths. Some people are amazing at doing certain things. I noticed something the other day while my girls were in my hair shop. Trinity was reading Allie's homework to her while Allie was styling Trinity's hair. At first I was going to say something to Allie about not reading her own homework, but then I smiled and thought, *Good for them for using each of their strengths to get their jobs done.* Trin has always been really advanced in reading while Allie has not enjoyed it as much, and Allie likes to spend time doing hair like her Mama while Trin does not.

What if we all used our strengths to help each other out in life to get the job done and to make other people's lives a little better? Let's use our strengths to help one another instead of comparing ourselves with others. Let's hope for the best in others and cheer each other on! Don't let the devil put the thought in your head that you are not as good as everyone else.

So at the end of the day, I chose not to be offended by this person's words. I gave it to God and chose to pray for the person instead. What if instead of talking badly about other people, we choose to pray for them instead? Maybe God will show us that there's a reason they act that way, and maybe if we show love instead of judgment, then their life will change. Here is my challenge—Matthew 5:44: "But I tell you, love your enemies and pray for those who persecute you."

Jesus, I place these people into your hands. I pray that you would bless them and that you would open my eyes to understand why they may act the way they do. I pray that I would learn to have compassion for difficult personalities and that, instead of talking badly about them with the crowd, I would rise to the challenge of loving all people. Amen.

66

LEADERS

Lately I've been observing leaders. I have been noticing qualities about them that make them great. We have all had that teacher when we were younger who we thought was the greatest, and they usually had the ability to be firm and earn the respect of the children without being mean. An example would be the coaches who have the gift of being able to push the kids and yell at them to work harder, then turn around and have fun with them later. This is also shown in the parent who knows how to be firm but also shows love at the same time; the pastor who oozes love so much that even when we need to be corrected, we can't help but still love them; and the boss we respect so much that we want to do whatever we can to please them.

I have always wanted to be everyone's friend, the nice person that everyone enjoys being around. I like to be the one who's there to give you a hug or a high five when you do something well. However, I learned on a recent trip that when I am buddies with the kids, the moment when it is time to go to bed and be serious, they have a hard time listening. I've realized that a good leader has to be firm as well, offering correction where needed. I've seen leaders take that power the wrong way, such as constantly yelling at kids without offering an ounce of affirmation. I read a quote by John Maxwell recently that says, "Leaders become great, not because of their power, but because of their ability to empower others." It seems to me that people get crushed if they are constantly being corrected but never praised. I really admire people who have that God-given ability to lead with a balance of love and firmness.

I think a good leader needs to be good at confrontation. I have realized that confrontation is always bad, and a good way to approach it is "sandwich" your message in love. I was fired from a job in college because I was scared to let them know that there was a conflict in my schedule and that I needed to miss a day of work. I was so nervous to call in that I simply didn't show up that day, which resulted in loss of the job. I learned my lesson after that, and I realized that it's okay to be afraid to say something that I still need to say—as long as my fear doesn't keep me silent.

We've all known a person who was doing something completely annoying. When that happens, I have some choices. I can go behind their back and say bad things about them until I get everyone on my side, I can ignore it and continue to get super annoyed, or I can confront the situation in love. Sadly, I hate to admit it, but many times I have tried the first two. But in learning to lead, I am watching people who confront well, and with the Holy Spirit's help, I am growing in this.

The quality I love most in leaders is when they lead by example and when their life is so passionate that people see them and want what they have. I was talking to someone yesterday who was telling me about the success of this diet she was on. She had lost a lot of weight and was excited about it. I couldn't help but ask her what she was doing for a diet because it was working so well in her life. It was a clear life change, and she was glowing as a result of it. A good leader is someone others want to follow because they want what that person has. Jesus is the ultimate example of that. Philippians 2:3 says, "Do nothing from selfish ambition or vain conceit. Rather, in humility value others above yourselves."

Father, I thank you for raising me up to be a mature Christian who is learning to grow in every area of my life. I pray that I will live my live in such a way that it leads people to you. Correct me in whatever areas I still need growth, and give me the strength to make those changes. I thank you for picking me up when I have fallen, so that I can be a leader in this life. Amen.

67

ALARM CLOCK

My daughter is the world's hardest sleeper, so I purchased the Sonic Bomb alarm clock with a device that you put under your pillow to literally shake you awake while putting off a sound that's loud enough to wake the neighbors. We decided a while ago that it would be good for her to learn to wake on her own because I believe that it teaches responsibility. Children learn to plan and anticipate things, and in reality, I was just a little worried that I would send her off to college only to have her sleep all day through all her classes. We have tried everything—including dumping water on her head (not our finest parenting moment)—so I hoped that the forty-dollar Sonic Bomb would do the trick. However, when it was time to leave this morning, she was still sound asleep. I couldn't help thinking that she might never overcome this huge problem.

Which brought to mind a lesson I have been learning about controlling my thought life. The Bible says in Philippians 4:8,"Finally, brothers and sisters, whatever is true, whatever is noble, whatever is right, whatever is pure, whatever is lovely, whatever is admirable—if anything is excellent or praiseworthy—think about such things." How often do we get frustrated with a problem and have a negative thought, only to have our minds run away with that thought and realize that our problem has grown? I think that, in raising children, we have a tendency to do this.

My husband Charles and I were on a walk a while back and I was struggling with a situation involving my kids. I was going on and on about this problem until it led me to another problem, and soon we had an outright dilemma on our hands. At that point, he told me to stop and name ten things that were going right with the kids. After stating those ten facts, I realized that my kids were pretty incredible. They are truly gifts that God has blessed me with, and focusing on the good things made those struggles seem pretty minor. So when those negative thoughts come rushing in, I stop myself, say no, and move on to the lovely thoughts.

I find that I have a lot more grace for those around me when I get my mind off negative thoughts about people. It's pretty easy to point out other people's faults, but now I realize that we are all a work in progress. Someone once said, "Don't judge me on the chapter of my life that you walked in on." We are all going through things and are at different points in our journeys; some are overcoming abuse from their childhood or other unimaginable events. Let's love people to life; stop judging them, stop pulling out the trash in them, and instead find the gems in them.

I'm pretty sure I'm not going to be perfect until I am face to face with Jesus! So until that day, I will control my mind. I won't let it lead me to anxiety. I won't get frustrated over the little things (like my kids sleeping too hard). I will be full of thanksgiving and praise! I will stop those bad thoughts in their tracks and get on to more growing!

Philippians 4:6–7 says "Do not be anxious about anything, but in every situation, by prayer and petition, with thanksgiving, present your requests to God. And the peace of God which transcends all understanding will guard your hearts and your minds in Christ Jesus."

Father, I thank you for your peace and for taking any anxiety that I may be carrying. I thank you for peace in my thoughts, and I ask you to help me to love those around me. Amen.

68

RESISTANCE BANDS

The other day, my niece and I started a new workout video. For the past four months, we have been meeting every day to do the same (very hard) workout video together. Neither of us has seen much progress from this video over that time, so we decided to change it up a bit last week. She picked a video for us that has weights and resistance bands. This past week I have been so sore that I am limping everywhere.

The last day we did it, I made the comment, "Everyone needs some resistance bands in their lives." Immediately I thought of a lesson on bulldozing fear. I just recently read a book on parenting that said one of the biggest problems in this generation raising children is that we are foreseeing possible hardships in our children and we are swooping in and saving the day for our children so they never have to go through any hardship or pain. I was totally guilty of this; I felt I was the ultimate helicopter parent, constantly swooping in and saving the day for my kids. I brought the forgotten lunches, the forgotten instruments, and made sure their world was a perfect bubble that was never affected.

The point when I realized it was really bad was when I was their team leader on a mission trip to Haiti. I snuck in and did their laundry for them when all the other kids had to do bucket laundry, and I even picked up after them before tent inspection to make sure their tent looked neat. At that time, I realized I was not doing them any favors; I was actually doing them a disservice.

I'm realizing in life that we actually need those "resistance band" moments for us to grow, those points where we look that problem in the eye and choose to bulldoze it instead of bowing to it. So now in my life, I love those moments when I realize I have grown a little: choosing to act in love when someone is driving me crazy, forgiving that person who is hard to forgive, choosing to keep my word even if it hurts, making the phone call that's hard to make, or choosing to catch that flight even when I'm a little frightened to fly for ten hours. I could go on and on about these fears that I am choosing to bulldoze instead of bow to. And in the end, I'm seeing myself grow into someone that is "unshakable."

We need to be a bold generation, to rise up and face our fears in the face, and to be overcomers! To grow stronger with resistance! "Consider it pure joy, my brothers, whenever you face trials of many kinds because you know that the testing of your faith develops perseverance" (James 1:2–3 NIV1984).

Father, I pray that you would peel back the layers of fear in my life and that my life would not be influenced by fear. I pray for boldness and strength to become unshakable. Show me the areas in my life where I have let fear sneak in, and I ask for your forgiveness for getting overwhelmed by these fears. I pray that your perfect love would cast out all fear. Thank you for never leaving me or forsaking me and for continually working in my life. Amen.

69

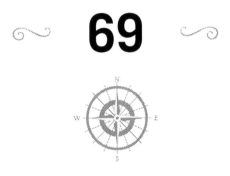

TREADMILL

Many people feel their lives are like a treadmill: going around and around, but not being able to get off it. Our lives are filled with jobs, kids, education, volunteering, and many other responsibilities. Many people are so driven that they feel that if they step off that treadmill, everything may fall apart. We have gotten so busy that we are barely living. We get so caught up in achieving, becoming perfect, bending over backward for others, coaching, leading, volunteering, and more that we forget what really matters in life.

Many times in my life, I have been guilty of living on this treadmill. I have been addicted to the word *yes*. I've lived many moments when I have had to cry out to God to restructure my life. I have been the person who volunteered for everything, coached, and served on every committee. I've been the person staying late for work because somehow my customer's hair crisis turned into my crisis. I've had to conquer my fear of letting people down. I always had a tiny hint of victim mentality where I felt that I had to do everything and that it was my job to help everyone. That was when it seemed that there was no way to get off that treadmill.

During this time of the stay-at-home mandate from the COVID-19 pandemic, I have been thinking a lot about people taking ownership of their lives. Many people have been living in victim mentality for too long. They feel that there is no way to change their lives; they can't have the life that they want, and they feel stuck doing jobs that make them feel miserable. Don't get me wrong, there are often times when our jobs are hard, and we should be grateful that we even have jobs. However, I'm talking about those of us that need to take charge of our lives now and go after the life that we want. What are the things in our lives that really matter? Do you value spending time with your family? We have had all this time at home to reflect on how we want to live in the next season, and I've discovered that I want to spend more time with my kids and with Jesus and put more energy into being creative.

I decided to set boundaries for myself. What activities am I volunteering for, and are they cutting into my family time? If I say yes to something, am I saying no to family time? Can I sacrifice some pay to say yes to my kids right now in this season? Can I learn to say no to other people's hair "emergencies"? How can we make small changes in our schedules to create a life that is less chaotic and more peaceful, with all our priorities in place? Don't live in victim mentality any longer; take charge, and get off that treadmill.

The Bible warns in Revelation 2 not to abandon the love you had at first for God. It says to repent and do the things you did at first when you fell in love with Jesus. Many of us have gotten so caught up in the treadmill life that we have forgotten to make God a part of our lives, let alone make him Lord of our lives.

What an awesome time to get back into the driver's seat of your life and take charge! Make your time with Jesus number one, make those memories with your family, sacrifice your time to pray over those kids at night, and do devotions. I have learned that I have to fight for time, and sometimes it's an all-out battle.

Father, help me step out of victim mentality and live a life that I enjoy. Help me get off that treadmill and spend my time on things that matter. Forgive me if I have abandoned my first love that I had with you. I pray that you would ignite that flame in my heart again. I want to live a life of passion and purpose. Show me areas in my life that I can let go or rearrange. Father, I recommit my life to you; I want to follow you all of my days. Amen.

70

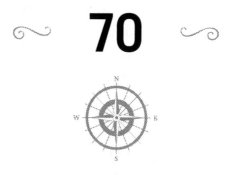

DATE BOX

My husband and I are coming up on our twenty-first wedding anniversary. A lot of people complain about losing the fire in their marriages the longer they last. Pretty soon, they are just going through the motions of day-to-day life without any connection.

The other day, I ordered something called DateBox online, and it reminded me of an important lesson I have learned in being intentional in our relationships. DateBox is a date in a box that gets sent to your house each month. In the box comes an activity for you and your spouse to do together. I thought it would be fun for us as a couple outside the usual routine spouses may fall into. It was a way that I could be intentional in our relationship.

I think many relationships are missing this. When was the last time you went out of your way to be do something special for your spouse? Even small things like making a special meal, acknowledging the other person with a kiss, planning a date, saying something kind ... anything that acknowledges the other person and says that you value them can make a huge difference. Many times, people feel forgotten and undervalued.

This is also true in relationships other than marriage. Many times, we are the ones waiting to be pursued. Looking back in my life, I've noticed that at times we need to be the ones who are selfless and pursue others. Be the person who invites others for a meal or calls others for a playdate or a walk. We need to keep the flame going by being intentional.

It's very easy to live a life that consists of going to work, coming home, and then getting on the iPad, but is it fulfilling? Specifically, are you doing things that help you build connection? Even if you are working on a puzzle together and not talking, you are still building more connection than sitting on a couch plugged into separate devices. Let's fight to build connection. Make a sacrifice for your spouse. Play together, dance together, and don't grow up and forget to have fun.

Father, help us love others well. Show us ways to be selfless and do small things to reignite our relationships. Help us to think of fun activities to do with those that we love. I pray that we never take for granted those around us, and give us boldness to step outside our comfort zones and invite others to do something fun. I pray that you would help us put a spark in our relationships. Thank you for the blessings in our lives, and I pray that we never take them for granted. Amen.

71

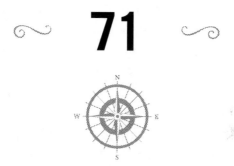

NO MORE SHAME

Lately, I've been thinking about things in my past that have left triggers in my life today. I was noticing that I have a hard time when I feel I am inconveniencing people. I seem to get agitated when I am wasting people's time, or I feel that I am asking too much of them. I struggle with letting people down, and learning to say no was a lifelong learning lesson for me.

Through my investigating, I learned that it came from lies that I had believed about being adopted. I was always so grateful that I was given a shot at a better life that I never wanted to be a burden on anyone. I believed all sorts of lies in my head—for instance, that I wasn't as good as everyone else or that I shouldn't be a burden. I also believed a lie that I was adopted because I wasn't wanted. This lie brought on a lot of shame.

With the help of a class that I took from Justin and Abi Stumvoll called Living Fully Alive, I learned to break up with shame. For years, I kept my secret of being adopted from my friends at school.

I thought they would judge me because I was different and not as good as they were. But when I finally opened up to them about it, they were super supportive. Just coming out and talking to them about it broke a lot of my shame right then.

As I got older, I realized that all those negative thoughts about my life were nothing but lies holding me back. I am learning to validate myself. I tell myself that I am powerful, I am wanted and chosen, and I have a lot of wisdom to share with people. I wasn't rejected at all; in fact, God showed his great mercy on me by putting me in such a loving and caring home.

What baggage are you bringing from your past? Were you bullied at school, and now you believe that you have no worth? Were you yelled at or even abused by your family? Did your family have money issues that have caused you to be afraid of spending? Did you go through a painful breakup that has left you with trust issues as an adult? Did your parents go through a divorce that has caused you to feel abandoned? Do you feel shame from something that you may have done as a child that you hid from everyone, convinced they wouldn't love you if they knew?

I'm here to tell you to break up with shame. Shame is a lie from the enemy that is holding you back. Replace those lies with the truth; declare out loud that you are valuable and that you are powerful. Declare that you are chosen, and that shame has no right to be a part of your life. Tell shame to go back to the pits of Satan where it came from.

Keep up the investigating in your life. What are the things that cause you to trigger? When those triggers pop up, it's important to ask yourself questions. *What is causing me to be so agitated? Is this something that I brought with me from my childhood?* When your frustration comes, just take a timeout, draw some deep breaths, encourage yourself, and validate yourself. Tell yourself things such as "I am so sorry that you had to deal with so much turmoil from your past." "I am so sorry that you felt rejected in high school." "I'm so sorry if your family life was a struggle." "You are going to break through this and lead a powerful life." "You are going to overcome shame and fear in your life."

Father, I pray for peace in my heart. I pray that you would replace every lie that I am believing and that you would replace it with truth. I pray that you would heal those areas in our hearts that have been bruised from past pain. I thank you for your mercy and kindness, which have brought me this far. I thank you for freedom. Amen.

72

PRESSURE'S OFF

I was thinking about a time when God taught me a lesson on giving. I have always had a passion to get my kids to all the church camps because I remember how much all those camps did for me as a kid. I would come back full of fire and excitement for God, so when my kids grew old enough to attend them, I made a point of seeing that they got to them all. They had such an impact on me that we even worked to help others go as well who couldn't afford it. I'm not saying that to show my good deeds, I'm just sharing so I can explain the importance of doing everything unto the Lord.

One time, we had sent some kids to camp and they came back full of excitement and stories. They seemed to have made some lifelong memories, and I felt pretty good about it—until one of those kids' parents came over and complained about the whole trip; the camp, the chaperones, and more. I sat there feeling defeated that I had paid for this, and she was so disappointed with how it went. I politely excused myself and went on a drive to blow off some steam.

I started talking to God and felt him speak clearly. It was Matthew 25:40, which says, "Truly I tell you, whatever you did for one of the least of these brothers and sisters of mine, you did for me." I felt great peace at that moment because this was God saying, *You gave unto me, and that was all that mattered.* The outcome was up to God. Our only job is to be obedient.

The pressure is off. Often we worry about giving to certain people because we are afraid that they will misspend the money. We worry that we invested all this money and the kids didn't get anything out of them, or that our money will go to waste. However, God is saying that the pressure is off because we are doing everything unto him. The outcome after that doesn't matter. We aren't giving to please others, but we give only to please God. He sees our hearts and our passion.

First Corinthians 3:6 says, "I planted the seed, Apollos watered it, but it was God who made it grow" (NIV). God is the one who makes everything grow. He is the one who encounters people, he is the one who rescues people, and he is the one who captures our hearts at camp. It's our job just to be planting seeds. We aren't going to make everyone happy. We may give at some point when people mismanage the money. But when we are giving unto the Lord rather than people, the pressure is off. Second Corinthians 9:7 says that God loves a cheerful giver.

Father, I thank you for the lessons you are teaching me. I pray that you will continue to give me wisdom and guidance in every area of my life. I pray that you will heal me of any lie that I have believed about money. I thank you for bringing others to water those seeds that I have planted in my kids. I thank you for causing the growth to happen. Amen.

73

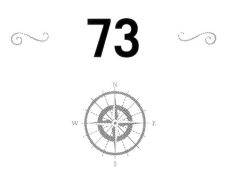

PSALM 91

Psalm 91 is a powerful passage to pray over your family. Lately we have been meeting together as a family before bed, and after we read our devotionals and pray, I have been declaring this. It has powerful declarations in it, such as "He will command his angels concerning you, and no harm will overtake you." Job 22:28 says, "Thou shalt decree a thing and it shall be established unto thee: and the light shall shine upon thy ways" (KJV). I'm including Psalm 91 in this book so you can declare it over your family as well.

Psalm 91

Whoever dwells in the shelter of the Most High
    will rest in the shadow of the Almighty.
I will say of the Lord, "He is my refuge and my fortress,
    my God, in whom I trust.

Surely he will save you
    from the fowler's snare
    and from the deadly pestilence.
He will cover you with his feathers,
    and under his wings you will find refuge;
    his faithfulness will be your shield and rampart.
You will not fear the terror of night,
    nor the arrow that flies by day,
nor the pestilence that stalks in the darkness,
    nor the plague that destroys at midday.
A thousand may fall at your side,
    ten thousand at your right hand,
    but it will not come near you.
You will only observe with your eyes
    and see the punishment of the wicked.

If you say, "The Lord is my refuge,"
    and you make the Most High your dwelling,
no harm will overtake you,
    no disaster will come near your tent.
For he will command his angels concerning you
    to guard you in all your ways;
they will lift you up in their hands,
    so that you will not strike your foot against a stone.
You will tread on the lion and the cobra;
    you will trample the great lion and the serpent.

TIFFANY DAVIS

"Because he loves me," says the Lord, "I will rescue him;
   I will protect him, for he acknowledges my name.
He will call on me, and I will answer him;
   I will be with him in trouble,
   I will deliver him and honor him.
With long life I will satisfy him
   and show him my salvation.

FAMILY BLESSINGS

Here is a blessing that I will pray continually over my family, and I invite you to pray it over your family as well. I also invite you to tweak it to fit your family. In the evenings, our family has been praying Psalm 91, but we personalize it. Instead of saying that no harm will come near you, we say that no harm will come near the Davises. We take that entire passage and plug our family's name in it.

The Bible says that the effectual fervent prayer of a righteous man avails much. I have made it my duty and privilege to continually lift up my family in prayer. You must be the one who is diligent. You must be the one who is willing to go into battle for your loved ones. You must be the one who won't relent.

Father, I pray that you will bless my children and my children's children unto a thousand generations. I declare that my children will be taught of the Lord, and great will be their peace. I declare that my family will grow to love God and to serve him. My family will walk in divine health and favor, and everything they touch will be blessed.

Father, I pray that you would radically pursue my family all of our days and that your presence would fill our home and the homes of my children. I declare that my children will never walk away from you but rather run after you all of their days. Father, use my kids to be a blessing to those they come into contact with. I declare that my kids will walk in supernatural signs and wonders and that their whole lives will be devoted to you.

In Jesus's name, I declare that every demonic spirit that has infiltrated my bloodline shall be cursed at the root and leave me and my family now. I declare that the fire of the Holy Spirit will destroy every lie that I have come into agreement with. I declare that my family members are conquerors and will live in victory.

I speak Psalm 91 over my family, that God would put his angels in charge of us and protect us in all our ways, and that no harm would come near us nor any sickness come near our homes. Bless my descendants with long lives and an excitement of life and energy to enjoy it. Father God, we praise you for all that you have done, for your provisions, your plans, and your protection. I thank you that you know every detail of our lives. I thank you that the blood of Jesus will destroy any demonic force trying to suppress my family's destiny. Father, I place my family in your hands and believe that you are going to do mighty things in their lives. Amen.

ABOUT THE AUTHOR

Tiffany Davis is a wife and mother of 3 beautiful girls. She lives on an island in Alaska where she spends her time working as a hairdresser and taking care of her family. She has spent years learning to encounter God during her day to day life.

Printed in the United States
By Bookmasters